GERALDINE CUMMINS:
AN APPRECIATION

By the same author

A Hand in Dialogue

GERALDINE CUMMINS: AN APPRECIATION

THE INSIDE STORY OF IRELAND'S GREATEST MEDIUM

BY

CHARLES FRYER

www.whitecrowbooks.com

Geraldine Cummins: An Appreciation

Copyright © 1990 by Charles Fryer. All rights reserved.
This Edition: Copyright © 2013 by Charles Fryer. All rights reserved.

Published and printed in the United States of America and the United Kingdom by White Crow Books; an imprint of White Crow Productions Ltd. in association with the Pelegrin Trust and Pilgrim Books.

No part of this book may be reproduced, copied or used in any form or manner whatsoever without written permission, except in the case of brief quotations in reviews and critical articles.

For information, contact White Crow Books
at P. O. Box 1013 Guildford, GU1 9EJ United Kingdom,
or e-mail to info@whitecrowbooks.com.

Cover Designed by Butterflyeffect
Interior production by essentialworks.co.uk
Interior design by Perseus Design

Paperback ISBN 978-1-908733-82-5
eBook   ISBN 978-1-908733-83-2

Non Fiction / Body, Mind & Spirit / Parapsychology / Spiritualism

Published by White Crow Books
www.whitecrowbooks.com

Disclaimer: White Crow Productions Ltd. and its directors, employees, distributors, retailers, wholesalers and assignees disclaim any liability or responsibility for the author's statements, words, ideas, criticisms or observations. White Crow Productions Ltd. assumes no responsibility for errors, inaccuracies, or omissions.

CONTENTS

1: INTRODUCTION 1
2: GROWING UP IN COUNTY CORK 5
3: THE YEARS WITH HESTER DOWDEN 11
4: THE YEARS WITH BEATRICE GIBBES 17
5: THE YEARS ON HER OWN 23
6: THE SCRIPTS OF CLEOPHAS 29
7: THE MYERS SCRIPTS 41
8: THE FAWCETT SCRIPTS 53
9: TWO UNPUBLISHED SCRIPT SEQUENCES 61
10: TWO EVIDENTIALLY-IMPRESSIVE SCRIPT SEQUENCES 79
11: INDIRECT PSYCHIATRY 91
12: THE COOMBE TENNANT SCRIPTS 101
13: REFLECTIONS AND CONCLUSIONS 115
APPENDIX: GERALDINE'S NON-PSYCHIC WRITINGS 131
BIBLIOGRAPHY: BOOKS BY GERALDINE CUMMINS 135
BIBLIOGRAPHY: BOOKS REFERRED TO IN THE TEXT 137

1
INTRODUCTION

I cannot be sure when Geraldine Cummins' name first came to my notice, but it must have been soon after my own interest in parapsychology was stimulated when I read an article in the Modern Churchman by John Pearce-Higgins during the autumn of 1968, nearly a year before her death, on the subject of psychical research and its relevance to the Christian hope of immortality. Afterwards, reading books in this field, I remember being impressed by *Travellers in Eternity*, in which was published a script-sequence which purported to set out the experiences after death of members of a family related to Geraldine's friend, Beatrice Gibbes.

Three years later I developed the ability of automatic writing myself, in a somewhat different mode from hers and (so far as the production of evidence has been concerned) of an inferior kind. My own writing of this sort is described in a short autobiographical work published some years ago; enough here to say that, while I believe it really has put me into touch with a real communicator (my father) it is nothing like so impressive as that of Geraldine Cummins.[1] Soon after this happened the idea came to me to write her biography, once retirement had given me the necessary leisure. The book has had to take its turn in a queue, but I fixed on 1988/9 for the actual composing so that it could be published in 1990, her birth-centenary year.

---

[1] *A Hand in Dialogue*, C. E. J. Fryer. James Clarke & Co., Cambridge, 1983.

One automatic writer writing about another may be expected to feel a natural sympathy with his subject, and I have certainly found this was so. We have shared, she and I, similar successes and endured similar frustrations. The typical psychic sensitive, whether on the spiritualist's rostrum, at the automatist's table or in the fortune-teller's tent, is commonly imagined to be quite sure of his or her own gift.

Some indeed are, and do not like to be informed that they are wrong. (Ena Twigg once gave me a very rough ride on this account.) All kinds of hindrances operate within one's head (if one may suppose for the sake of argument that this is where one's thinking goes on) which can add to, subtract from, distort or pollute the stream of information which the discarnate entity (if that is what it is) attempts to get across.

Then there is the further question, whether or not a buried part of the mind may not only distort and falsify, but even fabricate messages which to all appearances are originating from the minds of the departed. It seems to me, from my own experience, that this is more than possible, and that the part of oneself which dreams during sleep may also dramatise when one is awake and slightly dissociated. I do not know what Geraldine's dreams were generally like, though she admitted to having had some very vivid and occasionally premonitory ones. My own, certainly, are pretty good at providing pageantry and dramatic activity and manufacturing strange backgrounds. There is a dream - London which I regularly visit (chiefly in the vicinity of the Euston Road) and one of the schools at which I used to teach comes back again and again in unusual form, with different classrooms and playing fields; all are unlike the waking realities, but also self-consistent, so that each looks the same as before when I return during sleep. I have sometimes wondered whether in such dreams I am not entering into another person's memories. However, the occasional precognitive dream is presumably my own and not someone else's.

It is not so much the broad sweep of an automatically-written script that brings conviction as the small incidental and specific details which turn out later to be strongly suggestive of discarnate contact. To take an example from my own automatic writing: my communicator wrote that Geraldine wanted to tell me a few things. I was due to visit Cork, her home town, shortly afterwards, to do some researching among her papers and make enquiries among folk who had known her. Geraldine (if it were she) made two definite forecasts: one was for one of the people I was going to talk to, the other was for me. The first was an accurate statement of something that had happened to a bush in this lady's garden, which could not have been known or guessed merely from inspecting the garden; this, I think, was to afford conviction to that lady that her former friend was still around. The second was a statement about the door of the house in which she had been born, which turned out to be true. I think it highly likely that Geraldine was in touch with me on that occasion.

Nevertheless, being in touch with someone and receiving accurately communicated information from that person are not the same things. Geraldine was frequently sceptical about the material she received. Even when writing the scripts later published in her book *Swan on a Black Sea*, which simply reek of evidence of real communication with someone whom she had never met or known, she was sceptical. An attitude of doubt probably hinders a communicator from getting across; on the other hand gullibility may well cause a session to be swamped with junk from one's own subconscious and dramatising mind. It is probably inevitable that one will get a certain amount of junk, psychic flotsam and jetsam, which can never be quite eliminated.

One has to distinguish between two Geraldines during her lifetime. One was an active, intelligent, friendly, humorous, patriotically Irish and occasionally somewhat scatty woman, who had an ambition for literary success of the conventional kind, which she never in fact achieved, and the semi-entranced holder of a pen or pencil whom, to all appearances, intelligent entities other than herself made use of, to produce scripts on an astonishing variety of topics, views, sentiments and avowals which often conflicted with her own opinions and were sometimes of a quality she never managed to achieve when she wrote in *propria persona*. A dual personality, if you like, but definitely not of the Jekyll-and-Hyde variety, for I am persuaded that nothing she wrote ever did anyone the slightest harm, and there is no doubt that she comforted many recently-bereaved people and enabled psychological cripples to find a cure.

The scripts of which mention is made in the following pages are only a small fraction of all that she wrote, which in total are probably more extensive than the plays of Shakespeare. I have selected for comment, and in some cases for extensive transcription, some that seem importantly evidentially and others which particularly interested me.

I never knew Geraldine personally, though I wish I had.

This book is an attempt to appreciate her and her script-writing. Those who remember her may wish to take issue with me on this or that point. There have been other well-known automatists, but not, I think, anyone of quite her stature or with so great an output - in this country, at any rate. She is certainly part of the Irish literary heritage, along with Synge, Joyce, Yeats and Bernard Shaw. She is now *pulvis et umbra*: peace to her shade. Indeed, more than peace. I suspect she is still quite a busy woman.

2

GROWING UP IN COUNTY CORK

Geraldine Dorothy Cummins was born at 17 St Patrick's Place, Cork, Southern Ireland, in 1890, the fifth child and first daughter of Dr Ashley Cummins, a physician practising in that city, and his wife, née Jane Hall. There were altogether to be eleven children of the marriage, seven sons and four daughters, as well as some who did not survive infancy. Shortly before her birth the family moved from a water-lapped house on an island in the Lee to St Patrick's Place, a street which then housed well-to-do professional men and their families. It has since come down in the world; its buildings are now offices and headquarters of small businesses and look ill-kept and seedy. However, it would not be a great job to tidy them up, and one would like in any event to see a metal plate or stone plaque beside the door of No. 17 to indicate that a celebrated Irishwoman was born there. The house is fortunately still standing and one hopes that the developer will either leave the street alone or at least spare No. 17. Cork City is careful about its architecture and appearance; the horrors perpetrated in some British cities have not yet happened here. No skyscrapers have yet arisen. There are pleasant walkways, tree-shaded in places, along the banks of the Lee and its backwaters. The main thoroughfares are impressive - Grand Parade is as wide as O'Connell Street in Dublin - and multifarious little narrow shopping streets, full of character, criss-cross between them.

St Finnbarr's Cathedral with its three spires rises impressively on the south side of the river; to the north, on the hillside sloping up from it, the bell in the tower of St Anne's Church, Shandon, still rings the hours, though it no longer chimes before striking in the way which delighted the local poet:

> With deep affection
> And recollection
> I often think of
> Those Shandon bells
> Whose sound so wild would
> In the days of childhood
> Cast round my cradle
> Their magic spells.

The church is now closed, but it was here that the bells summoned the Cummins family with their growing tribe to the Church of Ireland service every Sunday morning, and tablets on the interior wall, to the memory of two of them, record the fact that they died fighting during the First World War, one in Gallipoli and one on the Western Front. Could she return to her native city Geraldine would find plenty still to recognise.

Dr Ashley Cummins, like his brothers, had chosen medicine as a career in his youth, and brought to it warm human sympathies and a naturally-combative Irish temperament. He was a champion of the underdog. According to Geraldine

> ... he waged for thirty years, among other battles for the poor, one against corrupt officialdom in order to get decent conditions for the thousand inmates in the workhouse hospital ... Because of his kindness and the special attention he gave to many poverty-stricken patients he was popularly known in Cork as 'the Poor Man's Doctor'.

She remembered him as an eager, impulsive, optimistic man, with keen blue eyes, in contrast to her dark-eyed mother, who was cautious and more pessimistic, with a keener sense of reality than her husband. On the whole Geraldine seems to have been more attached to her father than to her mother. Her former housekeeper recalls how, long after his death, she would often come in from strolling in the grounds of Woodville House, the Cummins' later home, looking as if she were in a dream and saying she had been walking with her father.

Dr Cummins - Professor Cummins as he became after being appointed to the Chair of Medicine at the University of Cork in his fortieth year, came (if family traditions were correct) of distinguished Celtic lineage. Sir Walter Scott, the novelist, had assured his great-grandfather that one of the latter's ancestors, of the Clan Cumainn, then living in Ulster, had crossed to Scotland taking with him the Stone of Destiny upon which later Scottish kings were crowned, and which was eventually, in the late thirteenth century, removed to England and placed in Westminster Abbey by Edward I after one of his punitive expeditions into Scotland. On her father's side, therefore, Geraldine was as Irish as could be. Her mother, on the other hand, could claim descent from the Anglo-Saxon royal house of Wessex. Ethelred, an elder brother of Alfred the Great, who had reigned briefly before him, had a descendant who emigrated from Cornwall to Southern Ireland after the Norman Conquest of England and founded the Aylmer family which established itself for many centuries at Kildare. From a member of this family Geraldine was descended through her mother. Another descendant had been Rose Aylmer, remembered now chiefly by readers of anthologies of verse because of the famous elegy written after her early death in India by Walter Savage Landor:

> Ah, what avails the sceptred race
> Ah, what the form divine,
> When every virtue, every grace,
> Rose Aylmer, all were thine –
> Rose Aylmer, whom these wakeful eyes
> May weep but never see,
> A night of memories and sighs
> I consecrate to thee.

But according to Geraldine she did not exemplify every virtue. Her early death was a consequence of being over greedy and eating too much pineapple at one sitting, though warned before-hand that it was a fruit to be consumed in moderation. She developed enteritis and, like the typical English King in 1066 and all that, Sellar and Yeatman's well-known skit on history textbooks, 'died of a surfeit in the usual manner'. It is doubtful whether Landor was ever told this. So Geraldine had a drop or two of English royal blood in her otherwise Irish veins.

After Dr Cummins had been appointed at the University of Cork he purchased a plot of land on a hill-top at Woodville south east of Glanmire, a village at the head of a creek leading from the River Lee five miles from the city, and built a large house there. While during term-time the family continued to inhabit 17 St Patrick's Place they spent their vacations a Woodville. The boys and girls here found plenty of scope for outdoor exercise, and played rough-and-tumble games in the grounds. Geraldine seems to have lacked the boisterous energy needed to keep pace with her brothers, though she took her turn in sawing logs with a cross-cut saw and in chopping wood with an axe.

She never attended any school. Her early education was entrusted to a governess who taught the whole family, but though her older brothers and younger sisters later received a formal education and continued it to university level, she herself was largely self-taught, spending hours at a time in the Public Library and reading voraciously - not a bad way of educating oneself, though the knowledge so gained is likely to be wide rather than deep and confined to matters that interest oneself. In her case it was Irish life and literature in which she immersed herself. None the less she wanted to follow her father in the field of medicine, but her mother dissuaded her and urged her towards a career in literature.

At the early age of seven she developed a passion for the Shakespearean drama. A certain Miss Mabel Mills had been appointed as governess to the young Cumminses; this lady was herself a devotee of the Bard and also had a crush on a certain Mr Rodney, a Shakespearean actor whose speciality was the part of Clarence, 'false, fleeting, perjured Clarence' in Richard III. The company of which Rodney was a member visited Cork and the whole family went to see the play performed. Geraldine immediately became an addict and learned long passages of it by heart. From time to time the children would recite and act out the parts they knew before their parents. Geraldine's own speciality was the ghost scene before the Battle of Bosworth Field where Richard III was to meet his doom. She would play all the ghosts in turn who appeared in the King's troubled dreams.

One may imagine her childish voice repeating:

> When I was mortal my anointed body
> By thee was punched full of deadly holes.
> Think on the Tower and me. Despair and die!
> Harry the Sixth bids thee despair and die!

Or the spectral appearance of Clarence:

> Let me sit heavy on thy soul tomorrow!
> I that was washed to death with fulsome wine,

> Poor Clarence by thy guile betrayed to death!
> Tomorrow in the battle think of me,
> And fall thy edgeless sword. Despair and die!

Perhaps it is not surprising that Dr Cummins and his wife decided that too much Shakespeare would be bad for her and unbalance her mind, so that a ban was placed on further visits to the theatre.

More suitably for an Irishwoman, she learned during her 'teens how to ride a horse, and followed the pack of harriers which hunted over the broken hill country east of Glanmire.

Later she became good enough at hockey to be chosen on one occasion for the Irish International team. Her younger sister Iris became even more proficient and played altogether in thirty-one international matches.

Not much is known of Geraldine's childhood and even less of her 'teenage years. We know only what she chose to set down in her autobiography and in one or two other books, and no one now remains whose memory can be drawn upon.

As she grew older she added to her literary enthusiasms a strong championship for the cause of Women's Suffrage, and with a like-minded friend she went around making speeches in its favour. On one occasion she was stoned through the streets of her native city by the same underpaid and overworked women workers whose cause she had espoused. She does not seem to have had any close male friends; at any rate she never mentions any. It may have been at this time that she determined to lead a single life.

According to her housekeeper Lillie Hall, in whom she sometimes reposed confidences, she decided that her mother's fourteen pregnancies were too high a price to pay for the advantages of marriage, such as they were. She merely wished, it would seem, for independence on a modest competence to be obtained from authorship, and this indeed she was enabled to achieve, though the kind of authorship which gained her repute was not the sort she would have expected. The writing that became her main concern in her later years was not that of a creator but of a transmitter. In the latter role she wrote millions of words. In her autobiography she expresses regret that she did not keep psychic work as a sideline and expend more energy on stories and plays; then, she felt" she might have done much better. Until 1914 she had no other intention. In June of that year, however, a chance encounter resulted in her forming a friendship with another woman, older and paranormally gifted, which was ultimately to re-direct her life and make her the twentieth century's most celebrated automatist.

3

THE YEARS WITH HESTER DOWDEN

Early in her twenties, after an initial foray into drama when she and her fellow-suffragette Susanne Day collaborated in a play which was produced at the Abbey Theatre, Dublin, Geraldine turned to the writing of short stories, and some were accepted by the *Pall Mall* magazine. The money she received made possible a continental holiday with her friend.

The two had just completed a tour of south-western Ireland, speaking on behalf of Women's Suffrage to mainly unappreciative audiences; feeling the need of some relaxation they then decided to go and view the sights of Paris, and booked rooms at the Hotel Normandie for a few days in mid-June, 1914. It was to be a turning point in Geraldine's life, since it was there that she met a talented and level-headed psychic medium who happened to be staying at the same hotel.

Mrs Hester Dowden, daughter of Professor Edward Dowden, was no fairground fortune-teller but a cultured and educated woman married to a Dublin physician (from whom she was later to separate, resuming her former surname) who had discovered she was an automatist. In a short and little-known book, *Voices from the Void*, published in 1919, she discussed this ability and its significance without putting it into a religious context. When she first began to receive messages through a ouija board she was inclined to think that she was doing no more than opening a window on her subconscious mind and that her automatism was simply a method of observing her own mentation.

As time went on she came to feel that there was more to it than mere introspection, and that . . . external influences of some nature work through us, using our senses, eyes, ears, brains, etc., their messages however being highly coloured by the personalities of the mediums. I feel sure that hardly any of the communications I have had are entirely due to subconsciousness. What the nature of these external influences may be is another and most interesting question and one still more difficult to answer.[1] The communications she received purported to come through controlling entities which operated the ouija board (or, in the case of automatic writing, her hand) when given the opportunity - sometimes one agency, sometimes another. The first to put in an appearance was Peter Rooney. In his first communication he said he was an American Irishman who had spent much of his life in prison and had eventually taken his own life by throwing himself under a tramcar. The scientist Sir William Barrett, one of the earliest psychical researchers, who was a friend of Mrs Dowden, made enquiries in the United States and discovered that a certain Peter Rooney had indeed fallen under a tramcar and been hurt - a coincidence so surprising in itself as to suggest that extra-sensory perception had been operating - but that he was still alive and had never had a criminal record. The entity Peter, on being reproached for giving misleading information, admitted that he had indeed done so, declined to give his real name, but none the less asked that he be allowed to co-operate in psychic experiments. Questionable though he may have been as an entity, he was none the less successful as a control, though he needed to be humoured. He specialised in such feats as correctly repeating quotations from printed books, which no one present at the sitting in question remembered having read.

A later control, who declared that during his earthly lifetime he had been a priest in Egypt during the reign of the Pharaoh Rameses II, and who called himself Eyen, was instrumental in developing Mrs Dowden's automatic writing. Unlike the plebeian and commonplace Peter he had qualities of culture and a vivid inagination, and wrote fictional material through her hand, but was in many ways unsatisfactory, being prone to flattery and falsehood. Eventually a third and final entity joined the band of controls, who claimed to be a Hindu woman. Unlike the two male entities she lacked imagination and a sense of humour, but she did not mislead. She was especially successful in

---

[1] *Voices from the Void*, page 4.

reading the minds of living people at a distance, and also had considerable powers of psychometry.

Whatever the facts may really have been about these entities and whether or not they had personalities distinct from that of the human being whose hand they used, they all from time to time certainly produced evidential information of which neither Mrs Dowden nor any of her sitters could have been aware unless they had telepathic abilities of a high order.

One afternoon during their holiday in Paris, when the weather had turned bad and sightseeing was out of the question, Geraldine and her friend agreed to join Mrs Dowden in a ouija board session in one of the hotel rooms.

It did not seem to be, at first sight, a success. Eyen came through and began to ladle out large quantities of doom.

Rivers of blood, he said, would soon flow in France. Many houses would be destroyed and a great number of people made homeless. Thousands would die. This, in the middle of June 1914, a couple of weeks before the assassination of Franz Ferdinand, heir to the Austrian throne, which was to light the fuse that led to the outbreak of the First World War at the beginning of August, and at a time when the international skies were clearer than they had been for some three years, seemed utter nonsense, and Mrs Dowden closed the sitting. Eyen was a notorious liar, she told her two companions. It seemed also possible that disturbed atmospheric conditions (a thunderstorm had now begun) might have contributed to the melodramatic pronouncements of the oracle.

A couple of months later they were all three ready to give Eyen some credence, and the chance encounter in Paris was the prelude to a friendship between Geraldine and Mrs Dowden which lasted for many years. The latter's home was in Dublin, and before long Geraldine, having found employment in that city, was sharing her house and being trained in mediumship. Just how the latter was achieved Geraldine does not say, except to observe that it was hard and dull work involving mental exercise. She soon obtained a control of her own, after Eyen introduced an entity who styled himself Astor, which, he said, had not been his real name during his earthly life, which had been spent in ancient Greece. He remained as her principal control throughout most of her life as an automatic writer. Mrs Dowden's description of him suggests she had a better opinion of him than of Eyen.

He professes to be the guide of Miss C., who lives in my house. We frequently sit together, and Astor appears invariably and opens the séance ... He is an intelligent creature, not given much to flattery - indeed very often plain-spoken. His leading characteristic is that he is clairvoyant and sees vivid pictures of the future ... He has predicted some quite unforeseen events in a most remarkable way. In one case he made what seemed a most rash and absurd prophecy about a business affair of my own, at which I laughed, I remember, but within a week this totally unlikely event came true. He is very clear in his statements, and does not hedge from being questioned, as Eyen does ... He is a much more rational creature than Peter or Eyen, generally ready to have his say and then allow others to speak; he is grave and moderate in tone, and allows no trifling on the part of the medium.[2]

Geraldine's own estimate of Astor, written many years afterwards, is somewhat less complimentary.

Astor is fiery and impulsive; I am cool and cautious, partly because of a lack of vitality. He has been frequently uncivil, even rude, in his remarks to sitters. In ordinary life I am over-civil, and I have not the moral courage to be rude to people when in my view they deserve it, or at least a severe snub. I therefore found Astor to be a very satisfactory supernatural godparent. He has a hot temper and bad manners, virtues which (I hope, so far) I have failed to cultivate.[3]

She made Astor's acquaintance first of all through the ouija board, but as her psychic ability developed, and she began to write automatically, his presence was signified by a distinctive style of handwriting, with large, strongly-formed letters, a hand quite different from her own. As to his independent existence, she was always a little sceptical and quite ready to accept that he might be a kind of secondary personality, exhibiting qualities of character and behaviour which she herself repressed. In any case he was merely an introducer of others. He spoke in contemporary grammatical English - a rather strange thing, one might suppose, in an ancient Greek, but no doubt the language, grammar, spelling and style derived from Geraldine herself, whoever or whatever may have been the entity that controlled her pencil.

---

[2] *Voices from the Void*, pages 20-21
[3] *Unseen Adventures*, page 23.

The awakening within her of a psychic ability seems also to have triggered off a propensity for precognitive dreaming.

Two of Geraldine's brothers who served in the British Army during the First World War were killed in action. At Suvla Bay, in Gallipoli, in August 1915, Harry Cummins died while leading an attack by Gurkha troops against a Turkish position. At or about this time, Geraldine recorded,

> ... I had a very vivid dream. I was running on an open plain. I saw the black faces of men in uniform who were running near me, each one a fair distance from the other, in an undulating line. This was new to me, as I had always seen soldiers marching in close formation on roads. My brother Harry was running a little ahead of us, urging us on. Suddenly he flung up his arms and fell forward on his face. Then I heard a voice saying, 'You will never see Harry again.' The experimental psychologist (myself) told me that it was caused by subconscious anxiety.
>
> Three weeks later we received the news that Harry had been killed instantaneously while leading his men in an attack against the Turks across an open plain in broad daylight ... The Turks were very good marksmen and easily picked out the white-faced British officers from among the dark Asiatic soldiers.[4]

Two and a half years later a similar dream forewarned her of the death of her brother, Captain Fenton Cummins, who together with his whole company was killed on the first day of the German offensive near St Quentin on March 21st 1918.[5] She was to have further death-warning dreams of this sort.

During the war years and for some time afterwards she worked in Dublin, occasionally returning to Cork, and was closely associated with Hester Dowden. She was ambitious for a literary career. The notion that she should devote herself mainly to working as a medium had not yet occurred to her; psychism was still a sideline, though an important one. Mrs Dowden's book makes it plain that Geraldine was one of the small

---

[4] *Unseen Adventures*, page 27

[5] Ibid., page 28. But some of her facts are wrong. The German assault was not on March 18th but March 21st. Also, it was not this offensive which put the Channel ports in jeopardy, but one a month later, mounted in Flanders.

group which worked with her in what one might describe as a psychic salon. It is not easy to make out what her attitude actually was at that time to her newly- discovered abilities. She professes to have been at first very sceptical and inclined to view them as by-products of her mental life. Even many years later when she could not deny that her automatic writing had provided evidence which strongly suggested discarnate origins, she was still quite ready to write off much of it as merely the outpouring of her subconscious mind. It seems fairly plain that religious feelings and opinions were not involved - at any rate, not consciously. One can of course make a substitute religion out of a belief in human survival of death; Spiritualism is (in the writer's judgement) such a religion. Geraldine never became a Spiritualist, but it would seem that she did come to believe that she had a mission in life, to comfort the bereaved by supplying evidence of the happy survival of departed loved ones. At cost to her own development and improvement as a writer of fiction she came eventually - largely because of the pressure put on her by a friend - to devote most of her mental energies to this end, though she did continue to submit her consciously-produced plays and stories for publication, and some did find their way into print.

4

THE YEARS WITH BEATRICE GIBBES

At the end of 1923, when she was still working in Dublin and closely associated with Hester Dowden, Geraldine met someone who was to alter the direction of her life and career - Edith Beatrice Gibbes. This lady, an upper-class English woman of independent means, unmarried and then in her middle forties, whose home was in Chelsea, had come to Dublin to consult Mrs Dowden, and in so doing encountered her younger associate.

Beatrice Gibbes was one of those people who feel they need to have a mission in life and who, when they have found it, hang on to it grimly like a dog to a bone. In her youth she wished to train as a concert singer, since she had a fine contralto voice, but her parents disapproved strongly so she gave up the idea. She came of a talented family; her grandfather had been a distinguished scientist and an acquaintance of the physicist Sir William Crookes, one of the earliest persons to be interested in psychical research.

She was fond of travel and her considerable private income made this possible; she journeyed widely abroad, had twice been round the world, and in June 1922 was elected as a member of the Royal Geographical Society. Something then happened which directed her natural curiosity into another field.

A close friend, a talented woman musician, was killed in a road accident. Sorrowing relatives raised the question, whether contact with her spirit might be made through a medium. In an attempt to secure such a contact Miss Gibbes arranged some sittings with Mrs Osborne Leonard, and these convinced her that she had been successful. Her interest in this aspect of psychical research was accordingly quickened. Indeed, she was now sufficiently interested to make it her principal concern for the remainder of her life.

However, she retained a critical attitude; she was hard headed enough to realise the need for caution and for examining supposed evidence with care. She knew that there were possible natural explanations for some apparently supernatural events, and that what appeared at first sight to be communications from the dead might really have been generated in the mind of the medium or transmitted telepathically to it from the sitter.

Her visit to Mrs Dowden and consequent encounter with Geraldine provided her with a mission in life which she had so far lacked. Impressed by the latter's now considerably developed abilities, she suggested to her that she should devote her time and energies to mediumship under, so to speak, her own protective custody. She need no longer be hampered by having to engage in gainful employment, but could reside in Chelsea, enjoy conditions favourable for functioning as a medium, share her friend's house, feed at her table and want for nothing.

Geraldine appears to have done some hard thinking about this proposition. The notion of being someone's psychic pet, a preserved channel on tap when required, did not entirely appeal to her. She had literary ambitions of her own, and the time and energy expended on psychic work might leave her insufficient of both to fulfil her vocation as an author (and in fact this did turn out to be so). On the other hand there were obvious things in favour of the suggestion. She was genuinely interested in her own psychic ability. Like Beatrice Gibbes, she was not uncritically-minded. She had been brought up to believe that convictions ought to be supported by observable facts, and the scientific bent of her father and brothers in the medical profession had reinforced that belief. She was by no means disposed to swallow psychism hook, line and sinker. What she used to term the 'experimental psychologist in myself' was always ready to offer non-supernatural explanations for the apparently supernatural. To allow herself to be stage-managed by somebody with an equally scientific attitude, who knew it was necessary to exclude, so far as was possible, circumstances from a sitting which might permit a sceptic to explain away everything which came across, would be a decided advantage. In collaboration with such a person she would be more effective than if she tried to work on her own.

Moreover it was certainly desirable (though not absolutely necessary) that when she wrote automatically someone else should be present, since on such occasions she was in a state of light trance and not fully aware of all that was going on around her. It would be as well for someone to be there who could replace filled-up sheets of paper with blank ones, substitute a fresh pencil when the existing pencil point wore down or broke, annotate scripts with details of spoken questions or comments, and generally ensure that everything went without a hitch. So far as devotion to the practice of the writing was concerned, her friend would be asking almost as much of herself as from her associate.

So in the end she agreed. The arrangement made was that she would reside with Beatrice Gibbes in the latter's London home, 25 Jubilee Place, Chelsea, for three-quarters of the year, returning during the summer months to be with her mother at Woodville. Her father had recently died and her mother would be glad of her company for a lengthy period each year, though others of her nine surviving children visited her from time to time. Most of her psychic work would be done in London, where her friend would arrange who should come for sittings or for whom proxy sittings might be arranged, and who should be excluded - and Beatrice Gibbes could be very tough-minded in excluding those whom she thought did not really need a consultation, or when she felt her friend was under too much stress. Visits to Ireland would be holidays from the psychic mill, though there was of course nothing to prevent Geraldine from doing automatic writing on her own while she was back at home, and Miss Gibbes could always contact her by letter or telephone if necessary. One notes that a proposal by one woman to another to set up house with her was not expected to raise any eyebrows; things were different then from now.

From Miss Gibbes' point of view the agreed arrangement gave her a purpose in life, exploring the next world instead of aimlessly wandering about in this one. Until now she had been a dilettante; now she was in effect the managing director of a concern, the publicist and to some extent the processor of the material produced through her friend's fingers. The potential administrator and executive within her now had something to do. She was aware of the need to provide Geraldine with the kind of environment and atmosphere which would not inhibit paranormal activity.

She knew that the evidentiality of whatever might come across depended to a great extent on her friend being kept consciously unaware of the circumstances which led to any particular enquiry. What a communicator wrote had not only to be genuinely obtained paranormally, it also had to be seen to be such. Not that all the care in the world which might be taken would necessarily prevent a critic from picking holes. That both women would firmly deny that they had looked up something beforehand was neither here nor there; had they been fraudulently collaborating, that was exactly what they would say. Supposedly honest people had been found before to engage in such deception. But no one who knew either of them ever supposed that they were a pair of cheats.[1]

Although the relationship at 25 Jubilee Place was not that of mistress and servant, with Geraldine being expected to make discarnate contacts on demand, a little quiet pressure seems sometimes to have been applied. Staying with her friend as her guest, she could not entirely ignore her wishes.

She herself believed that if she came to a case reluctantly she was less likely to receive genuine information. In general, however, she was willing enough. Many of her most convincing scripts came in consequence of Miss Gibbes' desire to enquire about some recently deceased relative or acquaintance. One book which the two produced between them dealt at length with the post-mortem experiences of members of a family related to Beatrice Gibbes. The years when the two collaborated at 25 Jubilee Place gave rise to an enormous volume of material which now reposes among the Cummins Papers in Cork City Archives. There were periods, however, when not much was written. At the end of 1931 Geraldine became extremely ill and had to have an operation, from which she recovered with difficulty. Also, during 1940-1944 she was doing some work of an investigative nature, which involved her

---

[1] An exception should perhaps be made here. E. R. Dodds, who later became Regius Professor of Greek in Oxford University, and was for a while President of the Society for Psychical Research, had known Geraldine in her Dublin days when he had frequented Mrs Dowden's seances, and by his critical attitude had earned for himself the soubriquet of The Universal Question Mark. He professed in his autobiography, *Missing Persons*, that he had his doubts about Geraldine's probity and thought she was not above cooking things up in order to soften the pangs of bereavement for someone she pitied. He once taxed her with this, and she denied it, but also added that, supposing she did, would that be so very wrong? He took this as an admission of guilt, but it seems much more likely that she was answering a sceptic according to his scepticism. Dodds had argued himself into a categorical denial of the possibility of human beings surviving death. In Geraldine, to use a Shakespearean phrase, his genius was rebuked. No doubt it would have caused him mental discomfort to have been willing to admit that there might be something in her supposed link with a world of departed spirits.

in a certain amount of danger and was undertaken from patriotic motives. This activity of hers has been alluded to in at least one published work, so for the sake of being comprehensive it is briefly mentioned here. One hopes that when her next biography comes to be written it will be permissible to publish her own account of what went on during this time. It is among the papers which she left when she died, and is at present in the hands of a Government department; for reasons of security it cannot yet be released.

During the war years, also, she spent a good deal of time away from London at her family's home in Glanmire, County Cork. Her mother was now very infirm and needed constant care and attention. There was also a farm to be supervised. So for a while she had her hands full. During what spare time she had she did a certain amount of literary work, typing while everyone else was asleep and often only getting four hours sleep a night herself. Occasionally it was necessary to take her typed material to Dublin; the journey from Cork can now be done in two and a half hours, but then took all day, since the steam locomotives which hauled them had to burn peat instead of the now-unobtainable coal; they had to stop long and often in order to recharge their tenders.

Geraldine was always worried in case something might happen to her mother on these occasions. As it was, the sort of accident she apprehended came while she was in the house. In a letter written for a group of friends she described the incident.

> My mother died at the end of October 1944. She had begged me to go to Church one Sunday morning. I was putting on my shoes in my bedroom when screams from the maids summoned me to her. She was on the floor, badly burned. She had got out of bed and her nightdress had caught alight from the electric heater. The maids had put out the flames with rugs, but she passed peacefully away two hours later, from shock alone, with me and one maid ... She suffered no pain. It was a merciful release after two years of bronchial attacks varied by three bouts of pneumonia. Her last words to me were: 'You have made me very happy. You have always given me hope.' This was, I think, a reference to the occasional sittings I had given her, for she implicitly believed in communication between the two worlds.

If it was a happy release for her mother, it was otherwise with Geraldine herself. During this period her own health suffered badly, and in September 1945, after her return to England, she had to undergo another serious operation, and again the recovery was slow and the convalescence prolonged.

Her association with Beatrice Gibbes came to a sudden end in December 1951. One morning the latter was busy correcting the proofs of a book about some of Geraldine's psychic writings and her friend left her to it while she went to visit an acquaintance. Returning in the afternoon, she found Beatrice had died suddenly of a heart attack. The shock was considerable, and for some weeks she felt quite unable to do any automatic writing or undertake any sort of psychic activity. She had been with Beatrice Gibbes for so long that the association had taken on some of the attributes, psychologically, of a marriage, and the pain of the unexpected bereavement was intense. She continued to live at 25 Jubilee Place, which had been left to her, along with much of the rest of her estate, by her friend, and eventually resumed her psychic work. Had she known it, her principal achievement in this field was yet to come.

5
THE YEARS ON HER OWN

Geraldine Cummins, now partnerless, continued to reside at 25 Jubilee Place almost to the end of her life, making regular journeys back to Woodville in County Cork. She did not lack occupation. Her psychic abilities were now widely known and she was often asked to exercise them.

Whereas Beatrice Gibbes had previously been the channel by which she was approached, which meant that a good many would-be consultants were turned away and only those of whom the latter approved were admitted, Geraldine made her own decisions now; her sieve was of a different mesh and perhaps admitted more. Until the end of 1951 she had also engaged in literary work of a more usual kind, writing occasional stories and plays for publication in books and magazines; however Miss Gibbes, a month before she died, had obtained a promise from Geraldine to give up all other sorts of writing and concentrate on psychical matters. There had evidently been some strain within Geraldine's mind over this. She harboured a natural wish to continue with her ordinary literary pursuits, and until the matter surfaced in some sort of argument with her friend in November 1951 she had deliberately distanced herself from psychical research (as distinct from the practice of her gift) since

> ... I feared that its technical jargon would interfere with my composition in regard to my consciously-composed literary work. I tried to

follow three pursuits - literature, experiments in transmitted writing, and, thirdly to attend to the mundane duties of a woman's life. It led to the distressing detriment of my literary output.[1]

The passage quoted suggests that, quite apart from her friend's urgings, she had reached a point where she felt she had to make a choice. She knew well enough that in her pursuit of conventional authorship she did not have an easy facility in writing; a few hundred words a day was all she could manage. On the other hand her automatic writing came swiftly and fluently. The first could at most give the reader a little entertainment, soon forgotten; the latter, she knew frequently brought consolation to the grieving because of its convincing quality, and had also been used to help the psychologically disturbed back to normality. The gift in which her mind was being used, by whatever agency, was obviously of more benefit to others than her own attempts to use her mind to satisfy her creative instinct. It could not have been an easy choice, but she made the promise to Beatrice Gibbes and felt obliged to keep it, diverging only once when she published a collection of short stories in 1959 (which may well have been written much earlier).

Her life style in later years appeared to her younger relations (some of whose memories I have been able to draw upon) as somewhat eccentric. In the words of one of them, 'she dressed appallingly, but was always very distinguished looking'. She seems never to have bothered what she looked like; personal vanity had never been an ingredient in her character. Walking around the streets of Chelsea she always wore the same small beret; when indoors she smoked a great deal, using a long cigarette holder. She never ran to fat, retaining a slim outline partly through exercise but also, no doubt, partly through smoking. When in London she obtained her exercise through playing tennis, at which for her age she was extremely skilful, particularly at doubles.

When in her native county she rode around on a cycle. She was fond of going to plays and the cinema, though as she grew deafer she preferred films with dubbed titles. One of her younger relatives retained an amusing memory:

> When she was in London she often had all her nephews and nieces going to her house, and she used to take them to a Chinese restaurant in Chelsea, and afterwards bring us to see a Continental film with

---

[1] Her last book, *Swan on a Black Sea*, page 156.

sub-titles, because when she got older her hearing became very defective, and it was quite amusing as if there were a film which didn't have sub-titles she would scream out, 'What's this?' and everyone would call out, 'Shut up!' . . .

Sometimes these French films she brought us to tended to be rather sexy; for example, someone was being married who was pregnant, and before the knot could be tied the doctor had to be fetched, and I remember her screaming out, 'What's happening?' Then I had to go into a long explanation as to what it was about.

Increasing deafness must have been a considerable nuisance to her, though perhaps it had its advantages when she was preparing to do automatic writing and 'concentrating upon stillness', by cutting out extra sounds. Her voice had always been a deep, rather booming one - so deep as to surprise those who met her for the first time - and she had deep-set, piercing eyes which were the feature people most readily remembered about her; they seemed to be looking away into some far supernatural distance. Many people in Ireland thought she was a witch. Those who knew her better were impressed by her kindness and understanding. She was a 'good woman', I was told repeatedly, by an Irishwoman who had known her well.

She had a circle of friends in London as well as in County Cork, and these included a few titled persons. Some of her family connections are, or were for a time, household names.

She had also, as was natural, many acquaintances among people interested in psychical research, though she herself never joined the Society for Psychical Research (SPR); she contributed articles and letters to that Society's Journal, and once addressed them at a private gathering on the subject of her automatic writing.[2]

She was never a religious woman in the usual sense of the word. Out of regard for her mother she attended Church of Ireland services with her while the latter was alive, but afterwards lapsed into non-attendance. She was certainly never a regular communicant. Not that she lacked a religious viewpoint of her own, but it seems to have been on the whole a vague one. Insofar as religion had anything to say about the survival of death - well, she had her own access to that particular sphere, and what she found there did not exactly reflect religious

---

[2] See the *Journal of the SPR:* May 1939, pages 62-75.

orthodoxy. One of her sisters was married to a Church of Ireland bishop, and there were definite reservations in that quarter about Geraldine and her psychic practices. For her, religion had no cultic side. She felt a dislike for St Paul, despite the fact that he was the hero of her Cleophas scripts, because of his supposed attitude to women. On the other hand, she felt that the same scripts had brought her nearer to an understanding of Jesus. Something like a sense of practical duty replaced religious feeling. She was motivated towards helping people in trouble, and sometimes, when writing automatically on behalf of such people, would feel an intense sympathy being generated within her. Her special sympathies were towards the Irish, particularly the peasantry; she was intensely patriotic in a non-political way. As to her own political views, they appear to have been conservative rather than radical, but with a small c.

She was patriotic in the manner that was customary with the Anglo-Irish of her youth, when Irish nationalism was growing and soon to become dominant. Her family, like other Irish Protestants (though there were exceptions) were attached to the Crown, and when the First World War broke out they followed the general Anglo-Irish trend. The men folk who were old enough volunteered to enter the armed services; as has been already noted, two of her brothers died in action. If one had lost kinsfolk in the fighting it would have been very difficult to feel sympathy with an Irish patriotism which favoured the enemy's cause and was prepared to use England's difficulties as its own opportunities. However, it was the latter cause which eventually triumphed in Ireland and gave separate nationhood to three-quarters of its people; the Protestant Irish accepted this with shrugged shoulders. It does not seem that Geraldine felt very strongly about this change one way or the other. Her pro-Irish feelings were for the Irish people she knew rather than the politicians and freedom-fighters.

In regard to her psychic abilities, her most remarkable performances were given during her later years. The last chapter but one in this book indicates how impressive they could be. However, she always retained a critical attitude towards her own ability. She knew non-psychic explanations could be advanced for much of what she wrote. She understood that what looked like proof of survival might very well be nothing of the kind if one took into account the mind's known powers of telepathy and clairvoyance. She herself dismissed her sequence of scripts, supposedly from the discarnate explorer Colonel Fawcett, as being no more than a mixture of information telepathically obtained with invented material from her own mind. Beatrice Gibbes had apparently believed in its authenticity but she herself could not.

A curious aspect of her detachedness was her reaction to the possibility of her own post-mortem survival. More than once she indicated that she would personally prefer extinction. Yet she had no doubt at all that life continued for others; her scripts all shouted this aloud. F. W. H. Myers, the psychical researcher of the late nineteenth century, had passionately desired to survive, but this is not a sentiment universally felt. The Roman poet Lucretius wrote lyrically about escaping from life's troubles into non-existence. Omar Khayyam looked forward contentedly to the prospect of turning down the empty glass when the wine of life had been drunk and the caravan started for the dawn of nothing. Not everyone wants pie in the sky when they die. Geraldine seems to have been in two minds about the whole thing.

Possibly she wished for extinction for herself and survival for those who wanted it. One wonders just how serious she was.

According to one of her cousins she was frequently aware of her father's presence, long after his death, when she was walking in the grounds of Woodville. Presumably she welcomed the experience. Would she have preferred nonexistence to the company of her father and mother and other discarnate friends? One feels that remarks such as 'the game is not worth the candle' arose from moments of depression.

In any case she was Irish and a certain licence may be allowed to the Gael in her. One is not on oath when making the odd remark.

With all her eccentricity and supposed unworldliness she was by no means unpractical. One of her younger kinsfolk reminisced as follows:

> My aunt always considered herself to be very poor, and one of her sisters used to 'pass her fivers'; she gave the impression of being terribly vague and unworldly, but she was totally on the ball. She left quite a lot of money; she got by very nicely. She gave the impression that she couldn't add two and two together and knew nothing about worldly affairs, but I think she was bang on the spot.

Her greatest feat as an automatic writer was the production of the Coombe Tennant scripts, published under the title *Swan on a Black Sea* in 1965. Not long afterwards her health began to fail and cancer manifested itself again. She returned to Woodville for the last days, where one of her cousins nursed her, and also gave up her psychic practices on the advice of a sensitive whom she respected, who warned her that in her weak physical state she would now be susceptible to undesirable influences. She died in August 1969 and was buried in St Lappan's churchyard on Little Island, close to her home, in the same grave as her sister Iris who had died the previous year. The stone is difficult to find and merely bears her name and the dates of her birth and death.

6

THE SCRIPTS OF CLEOPHAS

Soon after her removal from Dublin to London Geraldine began the production of a series of scripts which extended over some years and were published in a sequence of books.

They purported to originate from an early Christian disciple of the first century. An editorial foreword (the editors do not name themselves) prefaces the first printed series. According to its writers, who appear to have been clergymen:

> The narrative is transmitted through the 'Messenger', who is not the actual author. He demands from Miss Cummins mere receptivity and passivity . . . The whole attempt at communication is made 'at the bidding of a Holy one, Cleophas or Clopas,[1] who is, however, too far removed from man to commune with him'. Indeed, in this communication there are stated to be seven who are guided by Cleophas, and the 'ancient word' which they possessed in purity and integrity is shaped by them into a form in keeping with modern thought and expression.[2] The Messenger states that the chronicle he is now setting forth was known in the Early Church, though only a few copies

---

[1] A disciple named Cleopas is mentioned in the New Testament (Luke 24) as one of the witnesses to the Resurrection of Jesus. The Scripts, however, do not identify their author with this man.

[2] So the editors think; the modern reader would scarcely agree.

existed, and these have perished; but he also speaks of Cleophas as drawing from more chronicles than one, and of himself as fashioning the whole into a single chronicle ... Later communications from the Messenger have provided the interesting information that the original writings from which these chronicles are drawn were put together about sixty or seventy years after the birth of Christ, though certain portions are of slightly later date. Their authors were men who had themselves seen and heard the Apostles, and wrote for the most part at Ephesus or Antioch, using either Greek or, less frequently, Aramaic or Hebrew ...

The Messenger represents himself as one who in his lifetime on earth was a man of rather exceptional knowledge, especially of oriental languages, and at the present time is unusually fitted to utilise what he calls the 'heavy brain of man' to transmit his conceptions ... A singular point is that he seems unacquainted with the actual conditions of things on the earth: e.g. he does not know about the invention of printing, as evidenced by his insistence that 'scribes' should make many copies of his communications, and he admonishes us to be watchful 'as scribes make many errors'.

Later scripts from the same source give an account of the life of Jesus, both as a child and as a man before he began his public ministry. Taken together, the whole sequence of scripts forms the largest block of automatic writing on related themes which Geraldine Cummins produced. Even before their publication they had begun to attract attention from a few theologians who had got to know about them, notably Dr Oesterley, Emeritus Professor of Hebrew and Old Testament Exegesis at London University; on one occasion he went so far as to deliver a special lecture on them in which he spoke guardedly in their favour. Geraldine herself, though there were things in them which she did not much care for when she came to read them, seems to have felt that she should continue to co-operate in their transmission and that they were genuinely what they claimed to be. Psychical researchers, whose interest was in detecting their, so to speak, psi-content rather than in discovering new light on early Christian history, were less impressed than Dr Oesterley, as reviews in the Journal of the Society for Psychical Research show.

Though alone among psychically-written productions in their claim to provide information to supplement the Christian New Testament scriptures, *The Scripts of Cleophas* were not the only productions of their kind. *The Patience Worth* writings from the hand of the American housewife Mrs J. H. Curran, which began in 1913, are in many respects similar. This lady, born in the United States in 1883, of British parents who had settled there, had like Geraldine never received any formal education, and her knowledge of history was minimal and erratic. She had never taken any interest in Spiritualism or in any of its phenomena, but discovered when she was thirty that she could get a ouija-board to work for her. After a little practice communications began to appear, supposedly from the departed spirit of a young Dorsetshire woman who called herself Patience Worth, who claimed to have settled with her parents in America during the seventeenth century and to have been killed by Red Indians. Over a number of years, partly through the ouija-board and partly through words which she heard directly and wrote down, Mrs Curran produced something like three million words in story and verse, transmitted by this communicator and in different types of dialect but with a generally archaic flavour. Among her productions was an historical novel based on events of the time of Christ (and so to that extent resembling *The Scripts of Cleophas*) but avowedly fictional. Other writings reflected other periods of history. It was as if the surviving spirit of this Dorsetshire woman was overshadowing Mrs Curran, who said she had a definite sense of her presence which she describes as 'one of the most beautiful that it can be the privilege of the human being to experience'.

Geraldine's productions were different in that they came through automatic writing and claimed to be not fiction but psychically-transmitted history. The opening passage of the first of her Scripts indicates their intention and gives a taste of their style:

> I have come to give you knowledge of that wondrous time that followed upon the rising of Our Master. For a space the Brethren were sore afflicted and tormented in spirit. The pains of Hell beset them, but each kept this to himself and showed a cheerful countenance to the others.
>
> It was a time when the Eleven held themselves apart for much wrestling with the pitiless demons that beset them sorely. The Brethren were bidden by the Master to give much time to prayer and meditation, so that all might be made ready within them for the holy coming.

To revert to the *Patience Worth* scripts for a moment: one of the latter's characteristics was a mixture of antiquated English styles; indeed, sometimes they were in no recognised dialect at all but were an artificial construction whose manner was kept up consistently through the whole of the book in question. The latter feature also characterised *The Scripts of Cleophas*. They were given in a sort of modified Authorised Version Bible English, the language of 1611 rubbing shoulders all the time with that of the early twentieth century. Obviously no one ever spoke naturally in that manner. One might suppose the earlier element in the mixture represented the way the 'Messenger' might have spoken, were it not for the fact that he was apparently unaware of the existence of the printing press, so that if he had ever had a real earthly existence it must have been before printing was known, so that his English style would have been that of the fifteenth century or earlier rather than that of the seventeenth.

Supposing him to have been a real independent personality, one has of course to bear in mind that he could only convey his meaning through the mind and memory of the automatist, which might sieve out, add to or modify the thoughts initially fed in. Now Geraldine, who customarily spoke contemporary English in a slightly Irish way, had been subjected in her youth to lengthy periods of Church of Ireland religious services which in pattern and phrasing were almost identical with those done in England according to the Book of Common Prayer, and which always included lengthy readings from the Authorised Version of the Bible.

These occasions must have made some impact on her mind, even if her attention wandered as that of a young person is apt to do. One may imagine something like this happening: the 'Messenger', feeding his own thoughts into her mind, wished to clothe them in a manner appropriate to the present day, but also found in her remoter mental areas, where memories of her early churchgoing had been stored, seventeenth century words and phrases that he thought it would be appropriate to use, and which indeed he might have mistaken for contemporary usage. Hence the mixed style, a sort of emulsion of archaic and modern English, would emerge. But this is, of course, no more than speculation.

The Scripts of Cleophas were written automatically, in the usual state of light trance and in the manner described in a previous chapter, Beatrice Gibbes being usually at hand to change sheets of paper as necessary. On one occasion, however, the circumstances were otherwise. To quote from Geraldine's own account:

In 1925 I was invited by the late Dr Maude, Bishop of Kensington, to let him be present at a sitting for the writing of the Scripts of Cleopas ... Dr Oesterley of London University was also to be there ... On the ominous date when I entered the ecclesiastical study there were five clergymen besides the Bishop and Dr Oesterley present, and a thunderstorm began to rage outside. All the conditions were hopelessly against me, so the fear returned that I would fail to put myself into the concentrated state necessary to receptivity.

However, once I was established at a table with foolscap sheets before me, and had shaded my eyes with one hand while the other held the pen, a merciful tranquillity dominated me.

The seven learned witnesses were no longer there for me. After about three minutes the Messenger took over, and for an hour and a half an historical narrative was written at a considerable speed without a single pause. Sheet after sheet filled with writing was passed to the silent clergymen by the attendant sitter. It was a feature of this writing that there were no halts until the final full stop.[3]

    Two questions naturally arise concerning the Scripts. Were they really from an intelligent discarnate source, originating ultimately with someone who had lived in the first century? If so, can they be given parity of esteem with other records of the past such as the writings of ancient historians? The first question cannot be answered with one hundred per cent assurance in regard to any communications purporting to come from the dead, but in regard to utterances supposedly by the recently departed it is at least possible to check what has been transmitted against the memories of living people, or against written records, and some measure of evidentiality may conceivably be claimed.

    In the case of a communicator such as Cleophas and of the Messenger evidence of the truth of their statements can scarcely now be had. Even if some of the original writings from which the Chronicles claimed to be drawn (if there really were any) were to be unearthed, say in papyrus fragments from the sands of Egypt, it would be difficult to establish a clear connection between them and the Scripts which, as we have them, are admittedly only versions of the originals, not exact translations.

---

[3] *Swan on a Black Sea*, pages 160-161.

All the present writer would venture to say is that there seems some plausibility in the notion that some intelligent entity was trying in some manner to communicate a genuine portrait of his time. In support of the Scripts' authenticity much has been made of supposedly correct references to names and titles which only someone living in the first century or a learned Biblical scholar of the present day would have known. Dr Prince's examination of some of the Scripts, referred to below, shows that this is an unsafe argument. A little more plausible are the reasons given for some of the more puzzling problems of the New Testament: for example, why was the sin of Ananias and Sapphira, who (so to speak) fiddled their benefaction accounts, considered so serious as to merit death? Whether true or not, the reason adduced makes sense. Little things like this all add up, but to how much? Opinions will vary and I cannot myself see that the total is very great.

One simply does not know the extent to which the unconscious mind can fabricate and present in dramatic form stories which sound convincing - something which writers of plays and prose fiction (such as Geraldine herself) have been doing for hundreds of years, drawing upon their mental powers at all levels of their personalities. One's own dreams suggest that this ability is not confined to authors and playwrights; during sleep we create imagined environments, situations and happenings in which our own personalities become entangled and immersed, sometimes in a most bizarre manner. Can *The Scripts of Cleophas* be understood as Geraldine dreaming in light trance, building up images for herself in the context of stories heard from the lectern and pulpit of St Anne's Church, Shandon, and embroidering them with her own fancies and fantasies, the end-products emerging upon sheets of foolscap paper while her conscious mind was disengaged from the whole process? I personally feel that, while one must pronounce a verdict of non-proven in regard to the claims of discarnate origin, I do have a sneaking suspicion that there are real intelligences other than the automatist's somewhere behind the whole operation. However, this is more a hunch than a conviction. Wish-fulfilment may be operating, since I am a survivalist; were I the opposite my hunch might be different.

Supposing for the sake of argument that the Scripts did have a genuinely discarnate source; are they therefore to be regarded as a primary historical source, on a level with, say, Caesar's account of his invasion of Britain or Froissart's story of the Hundred Years War, which, making allowances for the writers' bias and partial ignorance, historians take seriously? Well, in the first place we cannot be sure that there was no deliberate intention to deceive. Conceivably the ultimate source of these communications was some mischievous entity like Bret Harte's card-playing oriental:

> Which I wish to remark,
> And my meaning is plain,
> That for ways that are dark
> And for tricks that are vain
> The heathen Chinee is peculiar,
> Which the same I am free to maintain.

    I am not really maintaining that some discarnate pigtailed stranger from Shanghai or any other trickster is really behind the Scripts, perpetuating a million-word leg-pull, though it is an intriguing thought. I think the likelihood of unconscious production is greater than that of infernal concoction. In neither case would it be genuine history. It is no indication of genuineness when names and references are produced which the automatist did not consciously know but which turn out when experts examine them to be true or apt. Quite apart from the possibility of telepathic influence or the clairvoyant reading of unseen written material, if it be true that one retains in one's mind all that one has ever seen, heard or read, while consciously forgetting the greater part of it, then Geraldine may have encountered these apparently evidential references at previous moments in her life, and they will have remained filed away in the recesses of her memory, to be retrieved later. And even if she had never read or heard of them, and the references were communicated 'from the other side' from a benevolent rather than a malevolent source, that does not necessarily guarantee their factuality. Such a communicator, like Patience Worth, may have simply wished to transmit stories founded on early Christian events, and the automatist may have misinterpreted their intention.

    One thing that might make the Scripts more plausible, as being highly probably of discarnate origin, would be the discovery within them of material which no one living at the time when they were written could have known, but which have come to light later. Perhaps some New Testament scholar who has the time and patience could be persuaded to undertake the very considerable task of reading them again, sieving through their soil for evidential nuggets.

If one is to suppose that an actual Cleophas, resident in some high spiritual sphere, really did try to enlighten us earthlings, then he must be a disappointed man, for since Dr Oesterley's time no reputable Biblical scholar has taken the scripts seriously. Geraldine Cummins' time, energies and talents would seem to have been wasted for a considerable fraction of her earthly life. She did not herself value these writings very highly, though she does seem to have regarded them as genuine. One thing which may have confirmed her in this belief was that at times they presented themselves to her partly as visions.

> When I record communications from educated people of the last decade I do not see images and scenes, but when I recorded the Cleophas writings, concerned with people who were said to have lived eighteen hundred years ago, I sometimes saw moving pictures of them and their surroundings. Among them were scenes of mobs and uproar, trial scenes or a mystical vision. Very occasionally a foreign word or a foreign name, Hebrew, Greek or Roman, appeared in illuminated images of it.[4]

Reviews of successive volumes of the Scripts, as they came out, by people interested in psychical research, were on the whole cool - at best guarded, at worst dismissive. If one may coin an Irish-ism, it is natural for a cautious researcher, as distinct from a devotee, to lean over backwards in an attempt to sit on the critical fence. As an example of such appraisal, A. D. Howell-Smith's review of *After Pentecost* may be cited: There is nothing in Miss Cummins' Script that may not be reasonably attributed to the operations of her subliminal self.'[5] He goes on to indicate a number of errors; however, it is fair to point out that if there were a Messenger using Geraldine's mind he would also have to cope with her misunderstandings.

However, the most damaging criticism came from someone who was acquainted with Geraldine and had respect both for her abilities and her honesty. Dr Walter Franklin Prince, an American psychical researcher who had had a theological training, contributed an article to a New England publication in which he subjected the so-called 'Third Parchment' of the Scripts to careful examination, comparing it with the text of the New Testament in the light of established knowledge of the

---

[4] *Swan on a Black Sea*, page 165.
[5] *Journal, Soc. for Psych. Research*, June 1944, page 69.

early Christian Church in its historical setting. He had the advantage of working from the actual script and not from a published version of it, and he notes that the editors had made a good many emendations in the latter; he obviously felt some distrust for them on that account. He came to the conclusion that this 'parchment' (and therefore presumably the others also) was historically unreliable, though he insisted that he was not in any way impugning the good faith of the automatist.

> I have corresponded and talked with her, and have been present at one sitting for the reception of these messages, and my strong impressions are wholly in favour of both her honesty and that of her friend Miss Gibbes. Indeed I frankly told Miss Cummins some of the most significant things I am about to say here, and admired her poise and calm, detached attitude ... So high is my opinion of Miss Cummins that I believe she will approve of this candid discussion and ... will agree that to ascertain facts is better than to maintain a theory. Any document put forward under the appearance of being an historical one must be ready to stand the tests. This is true for a sacred narrative, like the Acts of the Apostles, and it is true of a psychic one.[6]

Prince then goes through the 'Third Parchment' in detail and discovers thirty-six clear discrepancies between it and both the Scriptural narrative and also the other facts of this period of history as they were known in his time. The claim had been made (though not by Geraldine) that 'the internal evidence of the genuineness is sufficiently strong to bear the strain of the keenest historical criticism'. By the time he had finished his examination under the strong lens of his own acute intellect he had exposed that statement as nonsense.

His concluding remarks are worth quoting:

> We do not have to suppose that she is not honest in saying that she has never studied New Testament history, and the many and gross errors of which we have given some examples should protect her from the charge. But we do not have to claim for her what she has never, to my knowledge, claimed for herself. It would appear that she had not much acquaintance with the scriptural narrative when she began to write, but we do not know the quality of the scripts first received. She had produced, by her own statement, about half a million words all

---

[6] Boston Society for Psychical Research, Bulletin 10, page 44.

relating to the Early Christian Church by approximately the date her book came out (*Light,* April 7th 1928), and the book contains not more than 136,000 of these. It would seem that when statements about Jesus, Paul, Peter, etc., began to come there would have been an almost irresistible urge for her to look into the New Testament records to see how far the statements corresponded. I have looked in vain for any assertion covering this very important point, and in the absence of any shall take it for granted that the automatist did yield to that very natural curiosity. The trouble is that this practice, however innocent in intention, would have the result, with a very intelligent and keenly interested mind, of giving it considerable education in the course of writing a hundred thousand or so of words, and of educating the subconscious more than the conscious might be aware.[7]

It is possible that a good deal of pump-priming of the sort Dr Prince refers to, may have affected the material in the Scripts. However, from reading some of them (I have not, I confess, read them all) I do get the impression that an intelligence or intelligences other than Geraldine's had a hand in the production. For one thing, they were written very rapidly. For another, she was not allowed to know the contents of the immediately-previous script before she began the next one - yet they are clear and coherent, one following smoothly on another. Theological language and jargon, too, were foreign to her. If a part of her unconscious self had forced her conscious self to co-operate in a tiring and time-consuming exercise, exgurgitating material which did not much interest her - and as a matter of fact has interested few others - well, one supposes that the thing is possible, but why at such great length? Whereas if a real communicator were responsible it is easier to understand.

Allowing, then, for the possibility that a real discarnate Cleophas was behind the writings and a real discarnate Messenger piloted them through the recesses of her mental apparatus, are they to be regarded as historically true? That is another matter. I personally cannot dissent from Prince's conclusion that they are not. They may just as well have borne the same relation to History as Robert Graves' *I Claudius* bore to the Roman literary sources which he used.

They read convincingly, but so does Graves' novel. In that case, what happened to Geraldine resembled Mrs Curran's experience. Geraldine's productions were built round a skeleton framework of recorded

---

[7] Boston Society for Psychical Research, Bulletin 10, page 70.

events, while most of Mrs Curran's came out of the blue. There is no way of knowing, of course. Events in the first century could, in general, have happened as the Messenger claimed, and if he got the odd fact wrong, well, so did St Luke, that careful recorder, when he attempted to date the birth of Jesus Christ.[8] On the other hand, the whole sequence of Scripts may be fiction woven around fact. On that assumption Geraldine Cummins and Mrs Curran are entitled to divide the crown between them for what were on any showing astonishing psychic performances.

---

[8] Luke says that the enrolment order which was promulgated in the reign of Augustus, that all inhabitants of the Roman Empire should go back to their native places for registration, which took Joseph of Nazareth back to Bethlehem, happened when Quirinius was Governor of Syria. In fact Quirinius governed Syria some years after the death of Herod the Great, and we know from Matthew's Gospel that Jesus was also born during that king's reign. So the Nativity could not have occurred when Luke said it did.

7

THE MYERS SCRIPTS

It comes as something of a relief to turn from the Cleophas scripts to those which claimed to originate in the discarnate mind of F. W. H. Myers during the later twenties and early thirties, moving from a hotch-potch language to clear, correct and scholarly modern English, and from questionable historical narrative to an exposition of what everyone would like to know: what it is like to be dead, and through what stages one may expect to pass when that happens. The most important of these communications, according to the reckoning of Geraldine Cummins and Beatrice Gibbes, were compiled into two books, *The Road to Immortality* (1932) and *Beyond Human Personality* (1935).

Frederic W. H. Myers (b. 1843) was the son of a Lake District parson who died fairly young; his widow, Susan Myers, then moved to Cheltenham and sent her sons to the boys' public school there as day scholars. Frederic's performance in the classical languages, and especially in composition, impressed his teachers, and his ability in writing both prose and verse in English can only be termed precocious. In 1860 he went to Cambridge, and at the age of 18 gained a University prize for a poem. He seemed cut out for a career as a classicist and poet, though in regard to the latter he did not really fulfil his early promise except in occasional snatches. Like Wordsworth, about whom he later wrote a very perceptive biographical essay, he had a capacity for delight in the natural world, and joined to a first-class intellect a very emotional nature. He was the sort of man who aroused in those who had to do with him strong feelings of liking or disliking. Some thought him a *poseur* and hypocrite. A sympathetic account of his life and his work for psychical research, which neither overlooks nor overdoes his failings, can be found in Alan Gauld's *The Founders of Psychical Research* (London: 1968).

During his early manhood he fell deeply in love with the wife of his cousin, the Reverend Walter Marshall; she had formerly been Annie Hill, who came from a Yorkshire family. Soon after his marriage Walter began to show signs of mental instability and was eventually certified as insane.

Myers did all he could to help them, but the strain of looking after her husband, and perhaps other things as well, told on Annie so much that in September 1876 she took her own life. The event shocked Myers profoundly. She now became a sort of discarnate ideal for him, a Beatrice for his Dante.

His deep longing to rejoin her had directed his mental energies into finding out, if he could, whether the human soul survived death. Like many other Victorian intellectuals he had lost his religious faith, which the findings of geologists and biologists had appeared to make impossible if it was to be based, as was traditionally the case, on the Christian scriptures. But what the Bible and the Church failed to assure him might, he thought, perhaps be found through scientific enquiry into the mysterious and apparently anomalous happenings which, at their lowest level, appeared in the phenomena of Spiritualism.

In 1880 he married a young, beautiful and wealthy society woman, Eveleen Tennant, and for a while his longing for Annie Marshall was stilled, though never obliterated. The marriage was on the whole happy, though it had its stormy moments, since his wife was jealous of the memories he cherished and quite antipathetic to his interest in psychical research. In 1882 he and a number of like-minded men and women, all interested in the psychic phenomena which science was at a loss to explain, founded the Society for Psychical Research. He then devoted the greater part of his energies over the next two decades - that is, to the end of his life - to work for this body. He had a considerable income, partly salaried (he had become, like Matthew Arnold, an Inspector of Schools) and partly from investments, and enjoyed a good deal of leisure which allowed him to travel widely to carry out his investigations. His heart made him hope that the Society's researches would lead to a demonstration, independent of religious assertions, that the human spirit outlived death, but his intellect curbed his wishes. He was a careful observer of alleged psychic happenings and readily admitted alternative explanations if these were what the evidence suggested. For example, he had many sittings with mediums to see if he could contact Annie Marshall, and some of them he found impressive, but not till the end of his life did he assert that he believed he had at last reached her.

Along with his other literary work he collaborated with fellow members of the Society in writing articles and books on aspects of psychical research, and towards the end of his life he prepared and brought almost to completion his monumental two-volume study, *Human Personality and the Survival of Bodily Death*, in which he set out his theories about the soul and the subliminal self. This huge book is probably the most important single work yet produced under the aegis of parapsychology. He had nearly finished it when his health broke down, and it was found he had contracted Bright's Disease. A journey to Rome for treatment by a specialist proved fruitless, and he died in Italy after a long and distressing illness, impressing his doctors by the positive way in which he faced the prospect of death.

It may well be imagined that if he had indeed survived death he would wish to communicate and persuade his still living colleagues that he had done so. The 'Cross-Correspondence' communications which began a little while afterwards certainly look like such an attempt on the part of himself and some of his associates who had died somewhat before or after him. The scripts received by Geraldine, however, do not purport to demonstrate survival, but to describe it. Whether or not they really do so is a matter on which each reader must form his own opinion. To the writer, the view that they are substantially authentic appears a very plausible one; hence the space devoted to them in this book.

Sir Oliver Lodge, eminent both as a physicist and as a psychical researcher, had known Myers well. He contributed a foreword to *The Road to Immortality* in which he somewhat cautiously approved the proposition that the man he had known was the real author. Having read some of the original scripts before they were published, he wrote:

> On examination I decided that it was in many respects characteristic of F. W. H. Myers. The account he gives of the group-soul, for instance, is very much in accord with what he taught or discussed with me when he was here. So are the kinds of remark which he makes on the subjects of the subliminal self and reincarnation; they too are

sufficiently consistent with his views formed when here. And in general, though some of the things said are puzzling, or even superficially discomposing, and though, as he admits, they may not be absolutely correct, yet they are worthy of his intelligence, and if properly understood are instructive.

He chose his words carefully. He had himself reached conviction in this matter after losing his son Raymond in the First World War and subsequently receiving what seemed to him satisfactory evidence, through more than one medium, that he had survived death. In the foreword he tells how, through his son, he took 'Myers' up on the question of whether the recently departed did indeed live for a while in a world of illusion, as the scripts written through Geraldine asserted. The reply, couched in the familiar manner in which Raymond spoke, appeared convincing to him. The foreword ends accordingly:

> Thus fortified by independent testimony, I feel at liberty to commend this book as a serious attempt to give information about a future life, and the stages through which earnest people may expect to pass. There are lower stages for people less developed or less well-intentioned, but those are not here referred to. It must be very difficult for a communicator to give intelligible information about other states of being, in brief form, to folk with no experience of them, and there may be errors of interpretation, but I believe this to be a genuine attempt to convey approximately true ideas, through an amanuensis of reasonable education, characterised by ready willingness for devoted service, and of transparent honesty.[1]

As to the books in question: the first is quite short, with fewer than 30,000 words, the second a great deal longer. Both are concerned with what lies ahead for the journeying soul after bodily death. In *The Road to Immortality* the several stages are set out, together with their characteristic features, each stage more spiritually advanced than the previous one. The ultimate stage is union with God, though we are told that only a few achieve this during the whole span of human history. The immediate life after death repeats the experiences and qualities of earthly human life, purged from its previous grosser aspects. It is a transitory stage out of which the desire to progress spiritually increases,

---
[1] *The Road to Immortality*, foreword: pp. 9 and 15.

and the illusory paradisal pleasures begin at length to cloy and grow wearisome. So the transition is made to higher spiritual levels. A feature of this progression is the grouping of like-minded souls into co-operating companies whose separate personalities interpenetrate one another, though personal identity is not lost. A widening of awareness occurs which enriches the mind and is enormously rewarding. Between each of the different stages something akin to a death occurs.

Having sketched out the general pattern of progression, 'Myers' then gives details of what occurs at and after physical death, following this with comments on human faculties in general, such as free will, memory, sleep and telepathy. He more than once insists that there are things he does not know. I beg you to remember that I am but a fallible shade.' He speaks of himself as having reached what he terms the 'Fourth Plane' - i.e. that beyond the Plane of Illusion, the immediate post mortem level. He makes only occasional brief references to his own earthly life; one might have expected more, but there was perhaps no point in such harking-back; he was not now trying to transmit collectively organised evidence to show that he and his friends were still intellectually alive and kicking, but was acting as a careful expositor of discarnate realities, putting over difficult and unfamiliar concepts as well as he could.

At times, to illustrate his general account, he creates imaginary characters as *dramatis personae*, such as the lawyer's clerk, Tom Jones, whose progress after a life span of seventy years is traced through the plane of 'Illusion Land'. The end of the Tom Jones saga may serve to show his style as it appears in the first book:

> Nearly every soul lives for a time in the state of illusion. The large majority of human beings when they die are dominated by the conception that substance is reality, that their particular experience of substance is the only reality. They are not prepared for an immediate and complete change of outlook.
>
> They passionately yearn for familiar though idealised surroundings. Their will to live, therefore, is merely to live in the past. So they enter that dream I call Illusion Land. For instance, Tom Jones, who represents the unthinking man in the street, will desire a glorified brick villa in a glorified Brighton. So he finds himself the proud possessor of that twentieth century atrocity.

He naturally gravitates towards his acquaintances, all those who were of a like mind. On earth he longed for a superior brand of cigar. He can have the experience *ad nauseam* of smoking this brand. He wanted to play golf, so he plays golf. But he is merely dreaming all the time, or rather, living within the fantasy created by his strongest desires on earth. After a while this life of pleasure ceases to amuse and content him. Then he begins to think and long for the unknown, long for a new life. He is at last prepared to make the leap in evolution and this cloudy dream vanishes.[2]

A somewhat non-committal review of *The Road to Immortality* appeared in the *Journal of the Society for Psychical Research* in May 1933, more a summary than an evaluation of its contents. The writer was ready to concede that Geraldine had practically no knowledge of the work of the earthly Myers - something which is important in estimating the book's authenticity - but he does not offer an opinion one way or the other, though he mentions Lodge's favourable reaction.

The second of the two books, transmitted rather later, is very largely an expansion of the earlier one. It contains much more about what happens on the Third Plane, 'Illusion Land'.

After a few pages of eloquent but more or less irrelevant pleading that Western society should escape from its slavery to materialism, and the hankering for material goods, he devotes more than a quarter of the whole book to 'The Immediate Life after Death', emphasising once more its illusory nature and illustrating it by reference to the imagined experiences of members of a professional family who, at different levels of spiritual development, for a while fashion their after-death environment from their own imaginative resources before finding within themselves pressures to move either onwards or backwards. He also insists that there is what he calls a 'double' in association with every human being, a 'unifying mechanism' which accompanies each of us from birth onwards and gives a sort of continuity to the personality when it approaches and passes through the experience of death and assumes an 'etheric body'; the double's work is then done and it is shed like a husk. With the 'double' he associates that intriguing stuff ectoplasm, the stock-in-trade of materialisation mediums.

---

[2] *The Road to Immortality*, page 29.

> Ectoplasm may be said to be an intermediate substance, almost semi-physical in character ... The double distils and imparts ectoplasm, distributing it through the body, its ultimate purpose being the nourishment of the nerves and the enrichment of the cells. The substance may be possessed by certain rare individuals in superabundance, and such people usually find that they possess the gift of physical mediumship. Given certain trance conditions they can exteriorise it, and there have been mediums whose unifying body may be so mastered by a discarnate intelligence that the latter can cause the temporary disappearance of a part of the actual physical shape through its rhythm being altered, transposed into the higher vibratory rate of the double.[3]

There for what it may be worth, is his explanation of one of psychism's more bizarre manifestations.

'Myers' also has a good deal to say on the consequences of suicide (an act which his own son Leo was later to commit), distinguishing between justifiable and unjustifiable self-ending, and on the effects of sudden death, which hampers immediate development in discarnate existence. On the question, much discussed at present, of human reincarnation, he is quite definite that it happens.

> I am quite clear that those human beings who live almost wholly in the physical sense while on earth must be reborn in order that they may experience an intellectual and higher form of emotional life. In other words, those human beings I have described as 'Animal man' almost invariably reincarnate ... But metempsychosis does not involve a machine-like regularity of return. I have not noted any evidence of a continual progression of births and deaths for any one particular soul... The majority of people only reincarnate two, three or four times. Though if they have some human purpose or plan to achieve they may return as many as eight or nine times.[4]

And, a little further on:

> When a soul is born into a defective body it is due to the fact that in a previous existence it committed errors from the results of which it can only escape by submitting to this particular experience. The

---

[3] *Beyond Human Personality*, page 69.
[4] Ibid., page 76

apparently inhibited soul of an idiot, for instance, functions on the material plane and gathers, dimly, certain lessons from its earth life. Actually, such men as tyrants and inquisitors often reincarnate as idiots or imbeciles. They have, on the other side of death, learned to sympathise with and understand the sufferings of their victims . . . There is no set law concerning reincarnation. At a certain point in its progress the soul reflects, weighs and considers the facts of its own nature in conjunction with its past life on earth. If you are primitive, this meditation is made more through instinct - a kind of emotional thought - that stirs up the depths of your being. Then the spirit helps you to choose your future. You have complete free will but your spirit indicates the path you should follow and you frequently obey that indication.[5]

So much for the first half of the book. 'Myers' then goes on to describe, with several disgressions, life in what he calls 'Eidos, the Fourth Plane, the world of idealised form'. Here we meet the concept of the Group Soul.

When (the pilgrim soul) reaches the Fourth state, or world of Eidos, and is living consciously in the realm of pure form, he begins gradually to withdraw himself from ... his personality ... When on Eidos the soul gradually becomes this larger self, and before it leaves the Fourth Plane for the Fifth it is that greater being.[6]

He then considers the Fifth Plane, where human personality has been left behind. After some thoughts about the possibility of conscious life on the planets of the solar system (he asserts that such life either has been, is or will be found there) he proceeds to consider what he calls 'solar man'.

This is a new embodiment, not of the separate individual which has come from the earth and passed through the Plane of Illusion, but of the group with which the individual became associated in Eidos. Embodiment there must be, but in a body inconceivable to ourselves, vibrating at an enormous rate and capable of dwelling in the flaming atmosphere of the Sun or other stars, in a time quite different from our own. This is undoubtedly the most mind-boggling section of the

---

[5] *Beyond Human Personality*, page 79.

[6] Ibid., pages 97-98.

book, and 'Myers', recognising this, is both cautious and specific in what he says. The whole section, twenty-five pages long, an eighth of the whole book, is worth reading carefully and reflecting upon, if only because it is so obviously a thought-out passage. A lengthy quotation will not be amiss. It certainly smacks of the earthly Myers at his most lyrical.

> After the pilgrim has once more lived through the experience of Hades he is initiated into that remembered life within his group soul which has been gathered from planetary incarnation.
>
> He has harvested the intuitions, tendencies and fundamental characters of his group. He has yet to make the acquaintance of that extension of it which I call the psychic tribe. He chooses to be born on a permanent or stable star within the Milky Way...
>
> He assumes a fiery body... necessarily it bears no resemblance to the human shape. On Eidos he learned how to alter and yet to control his outward appearance... in stellar life he has developed and extended his imaginative and intellectual faculties to such an extent that he passes beyond human perceptive existence. With incredible speed his outward appearance changes, its astonishing transitions flowing rhythmically from design to exquisite design. In swift lightning flashes of ecstasy he vibrates in these successive bodies, thrilling and throbbing in a tremendous and brilliant world. Swept by solar tempest to the farthest limits of feeling, he becomes so vividly perceptive that he may be said to have reached a culminating plane of exalted stellar experience...
>
> Try to eliminate from your mind the natural human fear of flame and set a grander and finer conception in its place. Regard fire as the outward manifestation of a more exquisite and sensitively-attuned consciousness than your own. Reflect for a moment on the millions of stars that people the Milky Way, and then consider those other myriads of red, white and blue stars outside the galactic system, and ask yourself if it is indeed fantastic to suggest that they should be centres of manifested intelligent existence...
>
> Actually a far greater number of souls inhabit stellar realms; and if a detached spectator could view the Universe from the Sixth Plane he

would note that so-called human life is, comparatively speaking, rare, whereas solar life prevails in or is a commonplace of space-time.[7]

One naturally tends to be suspicious of writing like this and to estimate it either as the imaginative flight of a poet or the vapourings of a lunatic. When the book was reviewed in the *Journal of the Society for Psychical Research* by G. W. Lambert in February 1936 the latter was inclined to regard the whole sequence of 'Myers' scripts as derivative from other scripts offering descriptions of life after death, the implication being that Geraldine had read some of them and that her own scripts were a mixture of ideas taken from them. He seemed somewhat irritated that her 'communicator's lines of thought have been projected so far into the realms of speculation that they have lost almost every vestige of clue-forming material'. He also assumed that she had 'increased her normally-acquired stock of information about Myers since the writing of *The Road to Immortality*'.

Possibly she did, but it is equally likely that she did not (see the first paragraph of Chapter Five above).

The remainder of the book may be summarised by noting the chapter-headings: *Prayer, Hell, The right way of loving.*

They have a somewhat devotional tone. The second of these last three chapters has some interesting material; three passages are quoted below:

> It is necessary to discard the idea of punishment - a term which has figured very frequently in theological works of a past era when Hell was described by pious but sadistic prelates.
>
> Neither on earth nor in the afterlife are we punished for our errors. We merely experience the natural results that follow from a certain line of conduct ... Through Hell we pass to Heaven. Without Hell there can be no Heaven. The one is as necessary to the other as evil is necessary to good and good to evil ...
>
> The term 'everlasting fire' is utterly misleading ... The idea offends against the laws of nature. Actually the state we describe as Hell may be experienced intermittently with long periods of a most varied and, at times, pleasurable character in between. I speak for the ordinary

---

[7] *Beyond Human Personality*, pages 114-117.

individual ... who finally passes on to the higher regions beyond human misery and human pain ...

When I speak of the absence of Hell from the first state after death I allude to the experience of ordinary human beings. But abnormally jealous, selfish, cruel and crafty people do not always escape from the toils of Hell during their sojourn in the world of Illusion. Their own perverse natures interfere with the satisfaction of their desires; their incapacity for loving others in the true sense of the word defeats the law of psychic gravitation.

The doom of loneliness is theirs, so they tarry no very long time in this state, but seek a way to be re-born on earth.[8]

    I have quoted from the 'Myers' scripts at some length because for me they are more interesting and thought-provoking than any other of Geraldine's psychic productions except for the 'Coombe-Tennant' scripts which she produced towards the end of her life and which are dealt with in the last chapter but one of this book. One has to remember when reading both these books that they were produced when the writer was in a state of light trance, writing rapidly.

    Deliberate and conscious composition of an account intended to mislead is out of the question. Wherever one looks for an explanation, it is not to be found in the area of intentional fraud. Some personality directed her pen, and one not at all like Geraldine. It was highly intelligent and literate, possessed a wide vocabulary and was able to hold the reader's attention. It had a scholar's tendency to be circumspect, and the ability to produce at times a very poetic sort of prose which, like heavily-sugared tea, is not to everyone's taste. In other words, it writes very much as the earthly Myers did. Lodge was inclined to believe that it was his former friend. If one accepts that a man may survive bodily death and be able to perform in this manner, then surely the most likely possibility is that it was Myers. If one does not, then one has to postulate an entity who was living on this earth, who deliberately possessed Geraldine in this way and by a huge feat of telepathic interference transmitted these scripts - presumably just to amuse himself.

    If, on the other hand, we are to suppose that the automatist herself subconsciously framed all these writings, then what a remarkable

---

[8] *Beyond Human Personality*, pages 158-162.

character she must have been, able when her natural mental faculties were in suspense to impersonate with considerable plausibility the styles not merely of Myers but (as will be seen below) of many other people, including some she had never known. I find this more difficult to credit than discarnate influence. Possibly I have a bias in favour of the 'Myers' scripts because in many respects they chime in with what my own hand has written in respect to progression in post mortem spheres. Whether they are substantially true is one thing; many will be deterred from thinking so either by ingrained scepticism or by anti-psychic religious feeling which holds that all such communication is from the Devil and a deliberate attempt to deceive the credulous. Whether they are believable is quite another thing, and without wishing to suggest that they are infallibly oracular utterances (something I would certainly never claim for what comes through my own hand) they do seem to me to merit study and reflection.

8

THE FAWCETT SCRIPTS

While Geraldine seems to have accepted the Scripts of Cleophas and the 'Myers' communications as genuine discarnate disclosures, it was otherwise in regard to a series that began in 1935 and were continued and concluded between 1948 and 1951, which purported to describe the activities and eventual fate of the explorer, Colonel Percy Harrison Fawcett, after he and his two companions had vanished in the jungles of central South America in 1925.

Her opinion, given in the preface to the book in which they were eventually published, was as follows:

> As to the actual communications, written by me automatically without the intervention of my conscious mind, I have come to the conclusion that they are probably the product of my subliminal mind and a capacity for extra-sensory perception.
>
> The whole process of such supernormal communication is too mysterious for me to think of making any definite claim that these scripts were actually communicated by Colonel Fawcett.
>
> On the other hand, Miss Gibbes was quite convinced that the narrative was communicated by him and she was satisfied that she obtained sufficient corroboration to justify her view. I wish to emphasise that I make no such claim, and that I prefer that the reader

should form his own conclusions as to the authenticity or falseness of the record.[1]

Fawcett, like many other explorers, was a man who could not rest from travel. The unknown regions of central South America obsessed him. A glance at a world-atlas of the twenties shows that there were many unexplored areas here, with dotted lines indicating the presumed courses of rivers.

He had begun his career as an explorer during 1906, and during the next fifteen years he made seven expeditions, four in Bolivia and three in Brazil, as well as serving with distinction in France in the First World War, when he gained the D.S.O. In his book, *Exploration Fawcett*, written immediately before he set off on his final adventure, and published after his disappearance, he records that during twenty-four years of married life he had only spent ten with his family. Between 1921 and 1924, after returning from his seventh journey, he was continually uneasy and on edge, waiting for funds to flow in so that he might set out once more, this time to explore the upper basin of the Xingu, one of the chief tributaries of the Amazon, and search for relics of ancient cities built long before the time of the Incas, of which he had heard rumours when he had previously approached that area.

Eventually the money materialised, and at the end of 1924 he set out, accompanied by his eldest son Jack and a close friend of the latter, Raleigh Rimell. As the ship he was on neared Rio de Janeiro he wrote to his younger son, Brian, who was then working as a railway engineer in Peru:

> Here we are ... approaching Rio ... on the way to Matto Grosso, and with at least forty million people already aware of our objective. We shall leave for Matto Grosso in about a week, and Cuyaba [the last Portuguese settlement on their planned route] about April 2nd. Thereafter we shall disappear from civilisation until the end of next year. Imagine us somewhere about a thousand miles east of you, in forests so far untrodden by civilised man.[2]

Other letters followed describing in detail the journey into the interior by train and river-steamer, with living conditions becoming

---

[1] *The Fate of Colonel Fawcett*, page 10.
[2] *Exploration Fawcett*, page 178.

more and more primitive as they proceeded, and mosquitoes and other insects more and more of a pest. At Cuyaba they obtained horses and mules, and went into the unknown, accompanied for a while by native servants as far as the latter dared to go into a region of which they had a great superstitious fear. On May 29th 1925, the last letters were written from a point on the bank of the river Kuluene, one of the head-tributaries of the Xingu. They expressed eager optimism. Fawcett had heard more about the remains of old cities and was anxious to see them. He had been told that they lay to the north-east, and that before they were reached they would come across a high tower which the local tribes dared not approach because they believed it to be haunted, and after that a great waterfall.

No further word ever came about their subsequent movements, and for a long while no one expected any.

However, as 1927 wore on concern began to be felt. A search party went out but no trace of them. Then fantastic tales began to filter through, about Fawcett having actually been encountered by other travellers, about his son having married a native woman and having fathered a white-skinned, blue-eyed child; then, much later, a report that the whole party had been killed by arrows, according to the confession of an Indian chief who, somewhat later, when on his deathbed, changed his story and said that they had been clubbed to death. This chiefs successor pointed out where Fawcett had allegedly been buried. The bones were exhumed and sent back to England, but expert examination showed that they could not have been his at all. This was late in 1951. On that inconclusive note the story ends, so far as it can be ascertained through the usual methods of enquiry.

Much interest was taken in Fawcett's fate, and Beatrice Gibbes was among those who thought that mediumship might be able to supply information where human investigation had failed. She seems to have urged Geraldine to make enquires more forcefully than the latter found welcome.

Geraldine had a rooted dislike of Brazil which, she averred, caused her deliberately to avoid reading anything about it, since four of her kinsfolk had lost their lives in visits to that country. For Miss Gibbes, on the other hand, it was a land of mystery that fired her imagination, and she regretted that she was herself now too old to go and rummage in its jungles.

Eventually Geraldine consented to attempt a contact and the first sittings took place in December 1935. By now, though she may not have been aware of them, there had been five separate reports that Fawcett had been sighted, the last one suggesting that he and his two companions had been living for some years with a particular Indian tribe. It is a pity that we do not know how much or how little Geraldine heard of these sightings. Her own reluctance to concern herself with anything relating to Brazil would not have prevented her from noticing references in newspapers, and she might very well have absorbed and then consciously forgotten what she had accidentally seen.

Four automatic writing sessions produced a certain amount of information purporting to originate from Fawcett himself. At first it was not clear, either to the control, Astor, or (strange as it may seem) to the communicator, whether Fawcett was physically dead or still in his earthly body. Later it appeared that the latter was the case and that he was in a confused and dream-like state. The account he gave was that he and his two companions had been intercepted by a native tribe who, while not wishing to harm them, were determined not to let them go free. The tribal chief had given Fawcett the choice of their being immediately speared to death or of promising solemnly never to return to their people. Having opted to stay and remain alive, he, his son and Rimell were permitted a limited degree of freedom to explore their surroundings. The chief, who claimed descent from a white man, wanted Fawcett to marry his sister and become the father of a son who would combine the skills of the white races with the peaceable disposition of the native, and so be a suitable successor for the chieftainship. Fawcett had not found the notion attractive and had declined, but said that his son Jack had married a woman of the tribe and had had by her a daughter who had died and a son who had survived.

He further said that he had indeed found the remains of an ancient city, and that at the time when contact was made with him he was alternating between mental states in which sometimes his existing surroundings, and at other times the former life of the ruined city he had discovered, had been his environment. When in the latter state he was aware that he was living in the past, moving among people to whom he could not speak and who appeared quite unaware of his presence. He spoke of it as being another Egypt, an 'Alexandria of the West'. Here a Pharaoh sat on his throne and gave audience to petitioners while in the streets traders cried their wares and beggars asked for alms. At the next session he corrected the impression that it had anything to do with Egypt, asserting instead that the city was a colony of the fabled Atlantis, whose inhabitants had discovered the secret of what we should now call atomic energy, but which he referred to as 'blast electricity'. (It should be noted here that Rutherford did not succeed in splitting the atom until two years later, so it is unlikely that the notion of atomic energy being liberated had entered Geraldine's mind from outside, and equally unlikely that it was a product of her own fancy, since she had never studied Science.) In the third and fourth sessions he had much to say about the Atlantean civilisation, which had given rise to an empire of consciously superior human beings whose pride eventually led to their downfall and the destruction of their whole civilisation through the misuse of the 'blast electricity' which they had discovered. (A warning here for our own time, perhaps, but scarcely for the thirties of this century.)

The last two paragraphs summarise the material obtained during 1935. Whether or not it was simply the outpouring of a fiction writer's subliminal mind one cannot know. Beatrice Gibbes, however, thought she had obtained a certain amount of collateral corroboration. Between the third and fourth sessions she had attended a séance at which a medium of some repute unexpectedly produced confirmation of what Geraldine had written. The control announced that he wished to correct what had been stated on a former occasion. Fawcett was not dead but still living 'among a native tribe. He cannot get away. They make him amulet.[3]

They treat him well. He is with an Indian tribe.' But this of course could be explained (as Miss Gibbes must have realised) as the consequence of telepathy from the sitter.

During the fourth session, first Astor, and then the supposed Fawcett had more to say about the latter's peculiar awareness of a former ancient civilisation. He had been developing a psychic ability which enabled him to have direct knowledge of events of the past. First, Astor:

> His body lies within the hut, but for the most part his soul, in its etheric shape, wanders within the courts and temples of Atlantis . . . Yet in rare moments, when within his earthly body, he remembers his wife, his sister's home, and he tries to signal to them across space - but, if it reaches her, the message is only briefly expressed ... He will soon break wholly from his body and, once released . . . will rise into the etheric world of the departed.[4]

---

[3] This presumably means, They keep him because they believe he brings them good fortune.

[4] *The Fate of Colonel Fawcett*, page 32.

Afterwards Fawcett contributed a few words:

> I can't tell you whether I am alive or dead ... I am having a tremendously exciting time as layer upon layer of the ancient world is revealed to me ... I don't want to be discovered, as I take it that I can still be drawn back to the daily round of life if some adventurous chap starts out on another search. I don't want to be discovered and drawn back. I am far too absorbed and thrilled by this exploration of mine. It is the biggest thing I have ever been on. Later, when I have exhausted its possibilities, it will be time for me to look up London and the twentieth century. But when I am on a job I like to give my whole attention to it. I am slipping now - Fawcett.[5]

Thirteen years elapsed and another World War went by before Geraldine, again urged by her friend, made another attempt to contact Fawcett. Meanwhile other information had come to hand, some possibly genuine, from other South American travellers, and some through paranormal channels. To take the latter first: Maurice Barbanell, a noted Spiritualist, disclosed in a book that during sittings with Mrs Estelle Roberts one of her communicators unexpectedly spoke of Fawcett, saying he was a prisoner, alive and mentally well but physically in a bad state, that his son was dead and that he himself had become an 'advanced psychic'.

This sequence of sittings had been held in 1933, over two years earlier than Geraldine's first apparent contacts, but neither she nor Beatrice Gibbes had known anything about them until Barbanell published his book in 1940. At another of these sittings Mrs Roberts first said that Fawcett was dead, but later corrected this to a statement that he had been using his psychic ability to travel astrally, and that the medium had wrongly supposed he was dead. Somewhat later Barbanell was told that Fawcett had now died. All this (except for the latter statement) tallied with what later came through Geraldine's hand in December 1935. The question was, whether the latter might have already learned it, perhaps in conversation with someone who had been present at these sittings, and that it had sunk into her mind and been forgotten.

A further intriguing thread in the paranormal fabric was a statement by an author, H. T. Wilkins, who in a book entitled *Mysteries of Ancient South America*, published in 1945, mentioned that the explorer's wife,

---

[5] *The Fate of Colonel Fawcett*, page 34.

Mrs Nina Fawcett, believed that she had received telepathic messages from her husband which indicated that, in 1934, he was still alive but in captivity. This would harmonise with what Astor had told Geraldine, that Fawcett remembered from time to time to 'signal across space'.

In December 1948 the second series of writing sessions began, which lasted, on and off, until November 1951. In a sequence of twenty scripts ' Fawcett', now by his own admission discarnate, described his captivity up to the time of his death. After he himself, his son and Rimell had been captured they remained on good terms with the Indians for a while, and he had been able to investigate the ruins of more than one 'Atlantean' city, partly through excavation and partly through the psychic insights he had developed. His son had married a young Indian woman and they had had two children, a daughter who died and a son who survived.

His son and Rimell had eventually been put to death by the Indians, not out of ill-will but out of mercy to save them from torture and death at the hands of a cannibalistic tribe into whose territory they had insisted on going. He himself remained as a captive, treated with great respect. However, the fever-ridden jungle began to take its toll and he became very ill. When he appeared to have recovered the chief began to press him very insistently to marry his sister and produce a son. Sensing that the sister hated the prospect of such a union, though prepared to obey her brother whose command had the force of law, Fawcett decided to make an end of himself and died from a self-inflicted stab wound.

There are elements in Geraldine's automatically-written account which are possibly evidential if one supposes that she had done no reading or study about Fawcett, as she denied ever having done - and the writer is content to accept her word about this. The rumours and tales that filtered through between 1927 and 1951 are broadly in agreement with his having survived for ten more years, and the narrative reads very much like what he might have written, in its style and phrasing. However, if one accepts the possibility of telepathy one has to ask how much of the material might have been transferred from Beatrice Gibbes' mind to Geraldine's, there to be woven subliminally into a romantic tale which some film producer could have converted into a real box-office success. The lost cities, the forgotten civilisation, the noble savage chief with white blood in his veins, the friendly Indians, the honourable Englishman whose word was his bond, the notion of founding a dynasty from a union of white man's craft and native innocence - here were all the ingredients for a cinema film which could out-*Tarzan Tarzan of the Apes*. As it stands it makes good reading, and one disbelieves it, if disbelieve one must, with regret. It seems worth quoting from the final script, which came across only a few weeks before Beatrice Gibbes herself died.

> I have been thinking over the request that was made to me when last I paid you a call. [It had been a request for the names of persons and places associated with Fawcett's captivity.] The answer is in the negative. I feel I must keep my pledge made many years ago when I was with the Chief. I promised then not to bring 'White man scourge' upon him and the Indians by revealing the identity of tribes, etc., to any Western race, or indeed to any individual white man. I cannot therefore give you the names of particular Indians or the names of the various tribes.
>
> Here is my final message. For God's sake leave these Indians alone and let my bones rot in their grave. My head has been preserved, oh yes, but no explorer will ever find it. In the future, as in the past, Indians will only tell white lies about my end, if interrogated. They are under orders to do so, and they dare not tell the historical truth. For then they believe that the curse will fall on them - life after death passed in the Indian hell. . . White men deserve only to be told lies, in view of the past record of the whites' cruelty or corrupting influence in regard to the native population of South America.[6]

---

[6] *The Fate of Colonel Fawcett*, page 141.

9

TWO UNPUBLISHED SCRIPT SEQUENCES

Most of Geraldine's automatic scripts remained unpublished. Many who consulted her, of course, wished for complete confidentiality, and such script as was obtained would not be of much general interest. What matters enormously to grieving kinsfolk is of little concern to others unless the evidential features are really striking. A great deal of what Geraldine produced was of this kind. She saw it as an obligation to supply such material if it could be had, to console the bereaved by assuring them of their loved ones' survival. She did not suppose her ability had been given her merely to solve mysteries or satisfy curiosity.

Searching through the Cummins Papers in Cork City Archives, however, I came across two script sequences which were not in the 'grieving relatives only' category, and which deserve to be more widely known for their intrinsic interest. Each purported to originate from a man who had achieved a measure of fame during his lifetime. One was suppressed because Miss Gibbes did not want it published, the other because a promise was made to the communicator that confidentiality would be observed. Miss Gibbes having now been dead for nearly forty years, there seems no reason why the first sequence should not now be made public; as to the second, one may suppose that after half a century of silence the disclosure of information which was in no way shameful or discrediting to the communicator would no longer be subject to any sort of ban. Nevertheless I took the precaution, for what it was worth, of enquiring through my own automatic writing, and have received a *nihil obstat*.

The earlier sequence was produced during sessions held between November 30th and January 21st 1925. Geraldine was still a relatively young woman and had only recently gone to reside with Beatrice Gibbes. In the spring of 1924 an attempt was made to conquer Everest by a party of British climbers who approached the peak from Tibet by way of the Rongbuk Glacier and the North Col. Two men were selected to make the final assault: George Mallory, a skilled climber with previous Everest experience, and Andrew Irvine, a young Scot fresh from his university. After they had set out they were seen from a distance by another member of the expedition, climbing the north-east ridge and apparently less than a thousand feet from the summit; mist then hid them from view and they were never seen again.

There was widespread speculation as to whether they had reached the summit before perishing, and at least one psychic medium said they had in fact done so. Beatrice Gibbes had taken a great interest in the expedition, and wondered whether some news might be obtained through her friend. The attempt was made, and the typed copy of the first script was prefaced by the following note:

> The medium did not know of my intentions; the name conveyed nothing to her, and in my remarks I gave away as little as possible ... I was endeavouring to see if in time the communicator would mention the last climb, and say if he and Irvine got to the top or not, without mentioning to the medium in any way the information for which I was seeking. E.B.G.

To reproduce the whole sequence of the Mallory scripts would take up too much space, but it seems worth quoting extensively from them. The first three are fragmentary and confused and give the impression that more than one communicator was trying to get through. Scripts 4, 5 and 6, on the other hand, give a connected and informative account and include interesting and, at times, rather bizarre material.

Script 4

Astor. There are several near you to-night . . . [One is] a man who was here before and found it hard to speak.

E. B. Gibbes. Please let him do so.

Communicator. I want to talk. I am clearer tonight. You called me before and I was puzzled. I am Mallory. I am wondering if my people are known to you. I don't think they would believe I was alive. I am getting away now from the darkness I slipped into after that suffocating time. I can remember still the struggle for breath, and how the hammer seemed to go on beating in my head, knock, knock, and I wouldn't give in. I had got so far, and after the awful cold, I wonder, has anyone succeeded, or will anyone? I'd like to warn chaps not to try; it can't be done.

E.B.G. Don't you think so?

C. No, I'm sure now. I was very strong and fit, few could last like I could. I feel rather a fool now; after all, there were heaps of things better worth doing, but it was always my dream, Everest... I used to study it on the map when I was a boy. The trouble is, nothing can give the necessary oxygen, that's what beat me. I stuck out everything else.

E.B.G. Did you reach the summit, then?

C. Not quite. It rose right above me. I remember my despair. Oh, if I'd got to the summit and died I wouldn't mind, but I am just like so many others.

E.B.G. Do you remember anyone with you?

C. Yes, but I seem to have the last bit to myself; at least I seem to die alone. I think I was delirious at the end, everything danced about me and I had curious dreams. I wonder if Bruce will try again.

E.B.G. The subject is under consideration.

C. No, really, it's no good, they can't succeed ... It seemed to be possible when I started. I had my own theories about keeping fit. You know, I thought that the last bit could be overcome if one went at it slowly, got acclimatised, as it were. I ought to have made a dash for it but I was feeling the strain. It got fearfully cold, and I found that it was only by pushing on steadily I could keep alive at all, but I tried to husband my strength too much. I ought to have put on the pace more. I have only a vague recollection of my collapse and the torment in my mind. It wasn't death I feared, it was failure. Everest. It haunts me still.

E.B.G. I am a wanderer myself, and so was interested in the expedition; that is why I hoped you would be able to come and speak to us.

C. I understand. At first I thought this was some kind of devilry, a part of my delirium returned; now I know you are alive. Since I came out of the dimness I have been realising things, and people have come to me and told me that when I was rested I should go on to a new life.

E.B.G. I think you will, and will have plenty to do.

C. Good. I hate inaction, always did; when I had made enough money my idea was to explore. I tried, as you know, and bit off more than I could chew. I ought to have considered the possibilities more, but I hadn't a great deal of time or cash; the sight of the place was enough for me. I wanted to get going at once; you mustn't mind my bitterness. I expect I shall see things better later. Did they make much of a fuss about it?

E.B.G. Well, naturally there is much conjecture as to whether you succeeded or failed.

C. NO, I FAILED. [Capitals in script.]

E.B.G. Do you remember your companion?

C. Yes, we parted. I had to go on. I can't say what happened to him. May I speak to you again? I am losing hold. Goodbye.

Script 5

Astor. Astor is here. Do you wish to speak to the lonely spirit? I think he is near.

Communicator. Mallory. You told me I might come again.

I want to talk to the earth, and I am getting a clearer view of life and death now. It was all in a muddle at first; you see, I took a long time getting clear of my body. It didn't decompose rapidly in that great cold. I found myself outside it, watching the man that was myself and yet not myself, tied to him still by threads it took a long time to snap, perhaps because I was a pretty strong chap and died hard. You know, I believe people don't die when doctors pronounce them dead; they are still very often only just outside their bodies, as I was.

E. B. Gibbes. How do you know; have you studied medicine?

C. I am only speaking from my own experience. I was near my body for a long time after I died. I counted it by my sense of light, its coming and going; there wasn't much of a change in those misty places, but just enough to tell me. Do you know, I was so determined to live that if my party had come up I should have somehow got back into the dead body and made it live again, but they never came.

E.B.G. It was impossible, you know. Storms came up, and they could never have reached you.

C. I know that. But when we are dying we hope for miracles. Are they going to try again?

E.B.G. Yes, another expedition is talked of, but not for some time.

C. I think a little later would be better so far as the weather goes; we went rather too soon.

E.B.G. Is that so?

C. I am sure of it. The stiller weather comes later. I wonder if the school missed me much; you know, my old school where I taught.

E.B.G. I wonder what school that was.

C. Charter - I can't get it.

E.B.G. I know what school you mean. I had a brother there.

C. A good spot. Were you there?

E.B.G. No, he was long before your time.

C. He wouldn't be in my time, it was fairly recent. I wasn't there long. The boys, I think, were rather keen about what I went in for. Do they think of me now, I wonder? Tell them not to risk their necks at my game, it's not worth the candle.
Give me England, a sunny day, a cricket pitch and eleven beggars to wipe off the slate; that's worth living for. I didn't care much about it when I had it.

E.B.G. Have you any news of your companion?

C. We parted. I went on. I don't know what became of him. I thought I should meet him after death, one ghost meeting another, but I didn't come across him.

E.B.G. You meet other people now, I suppose?

C. People came and helped me, they broke the last threads for me so as to free me. They come spasmodically. I am told I needed a long rest. I died too soon, you see, so I've been like a bruised creature waiting for the healing that comes in the darkness.

E.B.G. I suppose they tell you of other worlds to explore.

C. Well, I have started on a new adventure, in a sense. It is difficult to explain mathematically and there is no physiology here. But a segment of me has gone forward, if you like to put it in that way. I mean I have been in a place of many colours, I have been conscious of my shape, it is not as difficult as you imagine, but it is very flexible. I have been learning how to control it, but these periods when I am not resting come to me as dreams come, and pass rapidly. I shall have this life permanently, probably, after a while.

E.B.G. Was there a precipice connected with your death?

C. It knocked me out, of course. I made a mistake, as you probably know, in the mist, and I slipped, caught hold of something, then slipped again. I didn't fall so far, but it broke something in my body, I can't quite say what; anyway, I couldn't stir, just lay there waiting, such a dreary time. I believe I was a bit queer for a while, all mixed up in my head, seeing figures and shapes; then that passed, mercifully, and I only felt weak and light, my body numb.

E.B.G. Don't speak of this if it upsets you.

C. No, I rather like going over it now, it doesn't upset me, I want to get at it as a whole myself. You see, for a while I had only fragmentary memories after death. That is very trying.
One longs to piece things together and one only gets glimpses. I remember my foot slipping, and the fall, the wonder, is this the end? The delight when I realised it wasn't, when I found myself alive and conscious on the ground. It was glorious to feel I hadn't been killed; for a while, you see, I thought my weakness would pass off and I would be able to get up and go on, but perhaps I shall find other mountains over here. I shall probably prefer the level for a while.

E.B.G. Tell us about those who came from the coloured place to help you.

C. They are very curious. I will try and explain how I perceive them. I know what I see breaks all scientific laws, but as I shan't have to argue about it with any of the old buffers who call themselves scientists I shall go ahead. They seem like long and pliable shapes that are shrouded, and change continually into different colours. They seem to float, or rather swim, without any exertion, in some strange buoyant stuff which they can pass through or can drift on. There is usually a kind of light with each of these beings, they seem to project that, and it gathers or sucks in thought and ejects it. I am afraid this sounds very tall, but through this stuff or fluid, if you look close enough, are tiny little ripples which remind one a little of threads. I mean each ripple has a sequence and a colour and suggest what is thread-like. I have noticed these ripples are made by what seems to be an intelligence. I conclude these ripples are the thought or speech of people; they have drifted into me several times, and I have been sensible of words framing an image or thought for me.

E.B.G. The medium is getting tired; will you speak again?

C. It is a great delight to me. I am on the edge of mysteries far stranger than Everest. Goodbye.

Script 6

E. B. Gibbes. Astor, will you ask the man Mallory to speak to us? He was here the other night but did not speak.

Astor. Yes, he will come. Wait.

Communicator. I was told I might speak. Herbert Mallory.

E.B.G. Yes, come and talk to us.

C. Thanks. I should like to. It's rather wonderful, to find the earth again; I haven't an idea as to what part it occupies in space now. I was interested in physics, as you know, and dabbled a bit in science on my own. Of course I didn't know much, but scientists would be absolutely staggered at the vision of earth as it appears, or rather doesn't appear, to us.
In the first place, to our own ordinary perceptions it isn't there at all. To our extraordinary perceptions it becomes visible. We only use them through an act of will. When I am in my ordinary state I probably pass through the earth, pass through human beings, mountains, seas, and I have not the slightest idea that I am travelling through matter. But I have learnt to adjust my focus to reach those conditions of mind when I can again make the earth seem real, and I can in your life even become associated with it again. It's awfully comforting.

E.B.G. It must be awfully nice to move about as you do.

C. It has its drawbacks. I had a pretty thin time at first, it wasn't all beer and skittles, [sic] Quite the contrary, I assure you. You know, all the same, Everest seems rather trifling now. I am rather glad I pitched into this life, it is really a most exciting place. When I was alive I had a horror of being fixed in a job for life. Fancy spending your life in a classroom. It's rather a waste of time, you know; that idea as much as anything made me want so badly to go out East and do something worth while before my little farthing dip went out. You make me tell you my thoughts; isn't it queer. I was a pretty shy chap, really.

E.B.G. Well, go ahead and tell us some more.

C. I'm not awfully interesting, you know. I was quite dull to meet.

E.B.G. Do you think, if another expedition is arranged, it will ever achieve its object?

C. No, no, it can't be done, the cold and the absence of air high up make it out of the question; no, no one will ever see the top of Everest and live. I didn't know what obstacles I was up against, really, and I always thought I could turn back. My pal went west, too.

E.B.G. Can you tell us anything about him?

C. He was done by the air difficulty. I don't think he was as tough as I. I had to part from him, you know; he couldn't travel at my pace, and I think physically he was the weaker man of the two. I have thought since, there is only one way by which Everest might be climbed, the scientist's way. If some of these experts would put their heads together and invent some kind of process by which we could continue to get enough oxygen, I believe there is just a chance.[1] Even then the climber would have to be a muscular Christian, [s/c] It wasn't the air trouble that knocked me out, it was the accident I told you of, but I couldn't have got to the top with the present kit.

E.B.G. It was the precipice, then, and not the lack of oxygen?

C. It was in a way both. I meant the rarefied atmosphere in conjunction with the other. I was sorry at first, it seemed mad to leave such a jolly sort of world, but I comfort myself with the thought that it's better than being stuck in a dull job. I always wanted to get on and find out. I loved enquiry for its own sake, and now that I am over the first shock I am getting my fill of it here. I say, did you ever climb mountains? The best sport in the world. I thought you might have tried your luck in Switzerland; that's a child's game, but I had some good times there before the mountains got too small for me.

---

[1] Oxygen-supply apparatus was carried by climbers on the 1924 expedition, but it was heavy and cumbersome. Possibly Mallory refers to it when, a few lines further on, he referred to 'the present kit'.

E.B.G. Will you wait a little while? The medium wants a rest. (An interval followed.)

C. Mallory. I am still a little slow at this telephone business. It's rather like telephoning; one never knows quite how much you get at the other end. You know, I'm awfully glad I can get on to you. Things have cleared up for me, since, so much. I've got free of what was keeping me in that confused darkness. A kind of husk, I think, has dropped off me since I began to think more clearly. Talking helps me to formulate my thoughts, a case of Q.E.D., Euclid, you know, the proposition proved at last. The worst of it is, if one proves one proposition in Euclid one has to go on to another. That's about what it means to me here.

E.B.G. Have you ever been in Egypt? I only ask because when you first spoke you seemed confused and mentioned that country.[2]

C. I was in Egypt once; I was there and I saw a part of it. I wonder, was that the time when the poor chap came who had been killed in some row out there? He saw you when I was trying to speak, and cut in, but he was puzzled by the light. I think he was trying hard to get through something; he made it impossible for me to go on talking. I was upset by it then; now I can understand better; he was probably very anxious to get through. Poor chap, I think he had only died in some violent way quite recently; he still had the sort of semi-material look. I can't explain it exactly, but I think from what I've been told it's like this. We are still dying when the body is dead, more particularly if we are killed in the prime of life, for though we do not suffer pain after leaving the body we are still kept near it by another body of ours which, though invisible, must die also before we are quite free.[3] His was still about him when he found you that night and tried to speak.

E.B.G. I can't think who it was; no one answering that description has spoken to us.

C. He was dead perhaps a month or two, killed, I think; he had that appearance, and was very anxious to get back to earth and tell his story. We all feel a bit like that at first; we imagine we are the first people

---

[2] The reference is to an earlier script, omitted here.
[3] One is reminded of what 'Myers' had to say about the 'double' in Chapter 7.

who have ever died and we want to talk of this amazingly terrifying thing to someone.

E.B.G. Does the name Yeovil convey anything to you?

C. I was there when I was young for a time, but Surrey was really my county. Yeovil, yes, I have people there. I have tried to put through to you any fragment of memory I could; my memory has been all in pieces since I died; the queer thing is that though I have moments when I remember most things in my life, there are others when my memory shuts off like a moving picture and I am in a blank. I think I shall understand myself better soon. I am helped of course by others who have shown me how to see without eyes and hear without ears.

E.B.G. The medium is getting tired; come and speak to us another time.

C. I should like to immensely; I may be clearer still. Goodbye.

Whether or not 'Mallory' made any further communications, I could find no further scripts. The reason why these were not made public was that Miss Gibbes, having been made a member of the Royal Geographic Society, feared for the continuance of her membership if her dabbling with mediums to satisfy her curiosity were to come to the knowledge of that august body.

The second sequence of scripts purported to originate from the surviving spirit of T. E. Lawrence, *Lawrence of Arabia*, the Oxford graduate and archaeologist who earned a military reputation for his work behind the Turkish lines as a leader of Arab guerrillas during the First World War, and later achieved literary distinction as the author of *Seven Pillars of Wisdom* and of a very readable prose translation of Homer's Odyssey. A man of strange and unusual personality, who never married, he tried in 1927 to escape public attention by changing his name to Shaw; he also, though he had been a Colonel during the War, joined the Royal Air Force as a ranking Aircraftman. In 1935 he was killed in a motor-cycle accident, and was buried in a church in Wareham, Dorset, where his tomb is surmounted by a carved effigy of himself, recumbent in Arab dress. A little over six months after he died the first of the following scripts was received.

Script 1

E. B. Gibbes. A pencilled note indicates that she had asked to be put into touch with Lawrence.

Astor. Yes, give me a moment ... I am ready. I think I have seen the Meteor. We call him the Meteor here. For he has behaved in an unusual manner since his passing. Very strange. After he had risen to the etheric world, having crossed the intermediate plane, he realised that he was dead to the earth. He had never believed in survival, but quickly he adapted himself to conditions here. But he was seized with one idea, a speculation [some illegible words follow] as solving the mystery of life, death and the Universe. He availed himself of the new powers ... and he has been flinging himself through space, testing whether in his belief space still exists, or whether there is no space for the discarnate being. He flashed to and fro, therefore, like a meteor, and we are amused by him, we elder spirits. Shall I call him? He will be difficult. Talk to him warily. Wait. He has consented to try and hold the control.

Communicator. Who are you? You mean you are what you call alive? What a curious belief of yours. You have no guarantee of it. I am all at sea ... I can't say offhand whether you are dead or whether I am alive. It seems you are one of the symbols of a dream I once had. I dreamt I was a figure that had an appearance called a man. This man was almost as complicated as a motor bicycle. He wanted to reach a goal. He was made for this purpose - that is to say he was made to travel at a maximum and minimum speed. His nature was a matter of gears with a high-powered engine.

Unfortunately for himself, after a conflagration called the Great War he had a collision with authority. His gears were damaged - the top gear, anyway. He then travelled on the lowest, but he couldn't, either when travelling on high or low, get anywhere. He came to the conclusion that there wasn't anywhere to go - that solution to his problem at any rate made existence possible. For then he became purely mechanical, living by performing a series of mechanical acts, dressing, eating, sleeping, devoting himself to work that made no call on his mind. He thought indeed that in this way he would prove that living was a sham. At any rate his distress about the thing he couldn't find became quiescent.

But then something incalculable happened - he went up in spontaneous combustion. Well, when you are reduced to old scrap iron you

TWO UNPUBLISHED SCRIPT SEQUENCES

naturally expect that that's the finish - no more flying through space, no more thought, no more stupid antics of human beings to torment; not a bit of it, the scrap iron went off into space with the velocity of the highest powered aeroplane that ever existed. It is still travelling - through endless worlds, times, regions, districts, localities, seas, oceans, darkness, by [word illegible] of stars, incandescent globes of flame that don't burn, great black monsters that appear to be solids and are not solids - he can't escape trying to escape all the time by finding an end, and maybe there is no end. But there must be somewhere; it's impossible, incredible that there's not a finish to every [word illegible] - the flag cannot come down, the revolver barks out the note that [word illegible] the end.

Queer, to see a woman again. I am awfully shy of women - always was - don't know how to talk to them. I can't get this straight. What are you, really? You don't know who I am, anyway . . . Damn it, what am I thinking about? I am scrap iron, that's established, anyway. Guess Shaw and all the others have forgotten me by this time. I don't mind telling you, then, that I took the name of Shaw. I can tell you everything because you can't interfere with me as human beings always did.

E.B.G. Pencilled comment: 'Called L. of A., then Shaw, Air Force, Dorset.'

C. That's my little place in history books, certainly. L. of A. retired to Dorsetshire, the public made wise about him during the War. To save himself he had to [word illegible] his own name. Now he is T. E. Shaw to you, please. Shaw, please. Is this an interview for the press? Give me your word, please, that you will not publish anything I write.

E.B.G. I promise.

C. It is most important. I will explain to you my real reason for wishing to be forgotten. It is one nobody on earth knows. It was caused by my meeting with an Arab - an old seer - it has to do with a very ancient knowledge. But first, your question. A letter, yes, that fool in Missouri - I remember he annoyed me.[4] Say that name.

---

[4] Possibly enough information is given in the paragraph which follows to enable an identification; I have not attempted to do this.

E.B.G. Pencilled but illegible note, evidently giving the name.

C. Oh, yes, I remember his letter - writer of books that were full of faults, but had such real feeling for the Ancient East I cared for them. Of course there was a lot of occult nonsense written about them, but there were fine passages that revealed life and those old ways of thought, so I wrote about the writer. I don't remember the names of the books now. If you meet the author, tell her (or him?) to cut out the acrimony and leave in those clashes of character, the queer bit about their belief in magic and the lovely lines that reveal that old world. The book needs editing, but they are alive, not dead, unlike most of the rubbish on the shelves of the library.

I was very interested in Eastern types - I wanted later on, when I had worked over the Arab seer's theory long enough, to write a book on the basic traces that were cradled in [word illegible] Egypt, Arabia, and show how and where this beastly modern muddle of human beings in Europe came in - it is a mess, you know - all of them at each other's throats, and most if not all mongrels, damned mongrels. I wanted to explode the idea of nationality by exploding the race myth.

There are no European races, no pure-bred pups. You follow me?

E.B.G. Fuller details later. [It is not clear what this means.]

C. Yes, but that secret, my secret. It was a strange experience. It came when I had finished my job - if any job is ever finished - out in Arabia. I was taken to visit an old man - an interesting-looking fellow, dark in colouring, characteristically an Arab - who told me first that I was going to be let down - my friends betrayed by my own country. Oh, you know all about it. Anyway, what I learned that mattered from my interview with this nameless man - he insisted on being without a name - that you keep losing identity, some precious part of your integral self, if you are in the limelight; millions of thoughts directed on you affect your unconscious, and unless you develop a technique of defence you are likely indeed to be robbed of a vital part, an independence of will. A sacred something that gives clarity to your ego. In other words, the applause of thousands and thousands, their thoughts all concentrated on your name, do in time, if you aren't careful, smash up what is really fine in you. It's as if a great wind blew, and the ever-burning lamp you see [words illegible] is extinguished by that common, dirty, gritty sirocco of the crowd, the massed mind. Do you believe in the Eastern magic?

E.B.G. Yes, certainly, in the seers.

C. Not the rubbish you get in the West - not that freak spiritualist jargon. I speak of the old principles that still mean something. Yeats [word illegible] up some of it for me.

But it is a known fact, as ABC is known to the English - it is known among the higher types of Arabs that concentration by the mass mind upon a name has the disintegrating effect I have described above. That's why I changed my name to Shaw - I had to have a name, unfortunately, but under the shadow of the famous Shaw I was safe. I mean, I didn't receive the mass concentration - he deflected it. But I had to do more, take up a life that consisted largely of mechanical acts. Those were cover, too. But when I wasn't leading an intellectually active existence I was less susceptible. No publicity.

Script 2

Astor. I think you had better quieten him by letting him speak.

Communicator. T.E.S. By Jove, this looks like London, and you too, you are real. I have a great deal to get off my chest. Oh, these fools, these damned fools of politicians. I'd like to scrap the lot of them. Well, I suppose I had better explain. I have been wandering among high, bare mountains [word illegible] with brown fighting men, I have been with lonely places of the earth again, back among those kind of men who are children, and who are to be eaten up and destroyed by white men. Arabia called me first, that's how I drifted back. The Arabs are worried - discontented - watching events sullenly in Abyssinia, and on the wings of their thoughts I travelled into the heart of Abyssinia. I have had a bird's-eye view of the situation, and I can assure you that if only the European nations will continue to supply Abyssinia and deny Italy supplies, then the Italians will in a short time be ready to set in motion peace negotiations.

There has been bad work in the Italian army out there, no one in Europe knows of it. But the fevers and the difficulties of climate have already more or less rotted the Italian army.

They can't conquer Abyssinia if things are not let alone by Europe. Let Italy eat grass [?] and in two or three months' time you will find that the whole danger will vanish -I mean of war in Europe.

Of course there's another side to it. Africa, except for South Africa, will later have to be recognised as the Brown Dominions. No white race can go in and boss the show without any way taking a bad loss. The best they can do will be to have a 'mind mandate' and advise and organise the natives in those vast tracts of country.

E.B.Gibbes. A pencilled note: 'Political crisis.'

C. Blind fools. No doubt they mean well. But if a mad dog is unchained, what do you do? You keep out of his way. He runs in a straight line for the nearest object that meets his eye and tries to get his teeth into it. If you are sensible you keep away from that straight line and you're safe. Europe is safe if their rulers realise this principle. Let them thank the gods or devils who look after them, that the mad dog made a B-line for Africa. Mussolini was determined, I knew before I came here, to fight someone. It is most unfortunate that Abyssinia was the victim; otherwise he'd have wanted a dog-fight in central Europe. His lust for blood must be satiated, so must the vanity of the Italians. Pray that they may be let alone and allowed to exhaust themselves among those terrific mountains. I have seen them, they're most alarming - like a Dante's Inferno. Your ignorant imperialistic Italian soldiers will look on them as the lowest hell before they're finished. They're shaking already. The fears of these governments of a war were absurd.

E.G.B. Pencilled note: 'Musso started [word illegible] and [word illegible] to alarm France.'

C. The French are like an old woman in a night-dress trying to hide herself under an umbrella. They're simple, filled with a thousand imaginary fears. They're quite hysterical. I am sorry if they infect Europe with the umbrella spirit.

E.B.G. Pencilled note: 'Political situation & [word illegible]. Origin of races.'

C. Yes, I had a big book in mind. I was going to write it with the supervisory help of B.S. Yes, he was to act as my critic, and I had in mind an opening chapter showing how race after race swept over Europe. Then I would pack in a good deal of historical data disclosing how the nations fused with the conquered people through intermarriage. I was

TWO UNPUBLISHED SCRIPT SEQUENCES

going to prove, for instance, that the Jews are an integral part of the German race. They have so intermarried with the Teutons Welt that all Germans should now be deprived of their [word illegible] rights because practically all of them have some Jew or Semitic strain in them. I believe I have, or rather had the clue to the lost tribes of Israel. These - who may be reckoned as few - wandered principally into Central Europe. So again the Teuton stock was enriched by the thing they hate - the Jew. In hating Jews they are hating themselves. Apart from that, a few were settled in Portugal. But here in England, too, we are a [word illegible].

The [word illegible] outlook has permeated or filtered through, mostly in France and England. Altogether this book would have meant the complete smash of the principle of nationality. I was going to write a chapter at the wind-up, full of thundering invective against the patriots in every land. Biologically speaking there are no races, no nations. I was going to denounce the principle of great nations and small nations. I intended to prove to them that the most civilised races, as regards the virtues, anyway, are the Arabians and Chinese. [Word illegible] the poet comes first, then the priest, then the merchant and lastly the soldier. The Arabs have a respect for human life and a system of brotherly cooperation that are far in advance of the Western system of grab-for-oneself and [word illegible] the under-dog.

All this I was going to put down in more polished language. I had [word illegible] public, biding my time, so that in solitude I might hatch out a bomb - in the shape of this book - that would explode with much force; human thought would be liquefied [?] from the bottom upwards, of course. Probably the governments would ban the book, for there was to be a very pretty satirical section in it, showing how white men comb out blacks almost invariably from the political arena. Further, I was going to prove that the nations of Europe and America are savages.

E.B.G. Pencilled note: 'Stop. Go now.'

C. Thanks. Queer I am not shy of you two women. Then, till our next time, if there is one.
T.E.S.
Lawrence of Arabia wiped out, annihilated.

It does not appear that there was another meeting.

10

TWO EVIDENTIALLY-IMPRESSIVE SCRIPT SEQUENCES

The scripts so far considered in this book were either ostensibly from persons in the remote past, evidence for whose historical existence could not be forthcoming, or from persons who, though Geraldine had not known them personally, had made names for themselves in one way or another, so that she might have gained knowledge about them through reading or hearing about them, before forgetting that she had done so. It is less easy to disparage or explain away the two sequences with which the present chapter deals, since, when the first contacts were made, she had never heard of either person.

The first appeared as a 'drop-in communicator' during a session when some of Miss Gibbes' discarnate relatives were communicating, and asked to be put into touch with a named person, validating her existence by giving some pieces of information which turned out later to be quite correct and which, if genuine discarnate contact be set aside as impossible, could only be explained if Geraldine's mind possessed an astonishing degree of super-ESP, ranging widely into the minds of people she had never met as well as some she knew, selecting pieces of mental material and combining them into a coherent whole in a manner for which no precedent exists. If this incredible ability may be supposed to exist, why boggle at survival?

At the time when these communications were received she was in a poor state of health. She had just returned from a long period of wartime residence in southern Ireland where she had been nursing her mother until the latter's death late in 1944. Despite her indisposition she made a few attempts to write automatically for her friend's benefit, and during a session on March 19th 1945 the following passage appeared in what her control Astor was saying:

> I must tell you there is a stranger here, a quiet grey-haired woman with a curious force . . . She says she died in Chelsea.
>
> She shows me a hand, that is her surname, I gather. Then a daisy. Yes, Marguerite Le Hand. She says she worked for a long time with an important public man - knew him well. She gives the name Frank. She says she wants to talk to David about Frank, and that David hopes to come to this town [i.e. presumably London] in April. If so, she begs that you see him for the writing, not to let anything interfere as she has something important to say about Frank . . . You may know in April, as David is likely to want to see you if he has time . . . That is all about her now. She doesn't seem able to give surnames. She seems to have been over here about three years. She says her message is important in regard to future peace.[1]

Geraldine herself, as was usually the case, was unaware of what she had written. Miss Gibbes, putting the name 'Frank' and the designation 'important public man' together, guessed that the American President Roosevelt was being referred to.

When the session was over Geraldine said she remembered something about David Gray; this latter was the United States Minister in Dublin, whom she had met more than once when she was in Ireland and who was interested in her psychic abilities; he also happened to be related to Roosevelt. So immediately after the communication they had some inkling of what the message might be about but none on the actual identity of the communicator. The statement that the latter had died in Chelsea misled Miss Gibbes, who naturally assumed that Chelsea, London, was meant, since she lived there herself, and she tried to trace locally the death of someone named Le Hand, but without success. However, her curiosity had been aroused, and at a session six days later she made a point of asking for 'the quiet grey-

---

[1] This and subsequent quotations in the first part of this chapter are from Chapter 2 of *Mind in Life and Death*.

TWO EVIDENTIALLY-IMPRESSIVE SCRIPT SEQUENCES

haired stranger you described the other day'. Further information was now forthcoming.

> She was an interesting woman with a keen brain, extremely quick but quiet, like one who had very great self-control and grip of herself ... She knows David Gray ... When I asked her who Frank was she replied that he was a man of affairs, and did not seem to wish to give more information. I said, was he in business, and she replied that he was the most important business man in his country... She seems to have had a confidential post with Frank ... David would know her ... She did not particularly wish that you should find out who she was ... That was her habit in life, to keep secrets, and so she was always reserved with strangers. [Miss Gibbes then remarked that she had not been able to find any reference to her having died in Chelsea.] She said, 'There is more than one Chelsea in the world,' and smiled.

The third communication from the grey-haired woman was, like the first one, apparently initiated by herself. She gave her name, Marguerite Le Hand, directly without recourse to symbolic imagery, said she had originally communicated because she wanted to warn David Gray that 'Frank was coming over', corrected Miss Gibbes' misapprehension by saying she had died in Chelsea, Massachusetts, commented on her successor's abilities - 'Ann is very clever but hasn't the experience', said again that she had worked for 'Frank' in a confidential position, and that 'Frank' was now resting, 'after the passage of death'. This was on April 14th 1945, two days after President Roosevelt's sudden death, which was of course generally known in Britain almost as soon as it happened.

It was now time to contact David Gray, and natural that Geraldine should undertake this since he and she were already acquainted. She wrote him a letter expressing her sympathy for him at the President's death, and added a note to the effect that a Marguerite Le Hand had 'called in March and was worried about something happening to a friend of his in April. She said she was from Chelsea, Mass.' It was necessary to write vaguely since correspondence was still being censored if sent to Southern Ireland, but she believed that Gray would be able to put two and two together, which he did. He replied confirming that Roosevelt had indeed had a secretary named Marguerite Le Hand, and that this lady had died about two years earlier in Chelsea, Massachusetts, and that, though relatively young, she had had white hair.

He asked if he might be sent excerpts from the scripts.

Beatrice Gibbes answered the letter, not by sending excerpts but by asking eight specific questions about matters mentioned in the scripts. To each of these he applied affirmatively and added three questions of his own, to be posed the next time she was contacted in a session.

At a fourth session these questions were put. The communicator seemed to wish to avoid answering two of them, which were about herself, but in response to the third correctly gave the name of her successor as secretary to the President - the highly unusual surname of Boettiger. She also mentioned a friend of the President who had predeceased him, giving his first name and the initial of his surname correctly. Gray was notified the results of the session, and in reply confirmed the correctness of what was said and expressed special surprise at the mention of 'Edwin W.' (He was actually General Watson, who had died suddenly on the ship which brought the President and his entourage back from the Crimea after the Yalta Conference in mid-February 1945.)

At the fifth session, on June 6th, further attempts to probe were made, but the communicator now appeared to become cautious and suspicious. However, she did give one remarkable piece of information: she communicated her second name, which few people knew and David Gray did not know. This was Alice.

Geraldine returned to Ireland for a summer holiday soon afterwards, and on June 20th had a session at writing with Gray and his wife at their Dublin home. This time Roosevelt himself appeared to come through, and beside the expected personal remarks added some trivial information of the sort that sitters often find singularly convincing.

> I well remember that last warm morning. I think it was horror at the prospect of a detestable lunch of gruel that made me collapse ... I was very active at my funeral, and the only one who paid attention to me was Scottie, my dog ... When my dog saw me he rolled on the ground, making quite a bit of diversion. But nobody guessed he rolled on the grass with joy because he saw me.

It had been a nice morning, the President had had gruel just before his lunch (a food which he indeed did not relish) and the dog was a Scotch terrier who was in the habit of rolling over when meeting someone he liked.

It was not possible to continue this intriguing investigation since Geraldine had to go into hospital for a serious operation which was followed by a long period of convalescence. The case was reported in the *Journal of the Society of Psychical Research* for May 1947, with assumed names being substituted for the real ones. Enough facts had certainly been correctly conveyed, facts all of which were unknown to Geraldine and Beatrice Gibbes and some also to David Gray, to make it almost impossible to suppose that their production was the consequence of chance guesswork.

One may surely also rule out the suggestion of a conspiracy to deceive the world (or that small part of the world which is interested in psychic disclosures) on the parts of those three persons. Had ESP between living persons not been established as a fact, the likelihood of there having been discarnate contact would have been overwhelmingly great.

As it is, if it were a telepathic tour de force it involved astonishing psychic virtuosity. Is it really believable that a middle aged woman of moderate educational attainments (though considerable intelligence) who was in a poor state of health, with a cancer which needed removing, had the mental agility to reach out at incredible speed across the oceans, and select from the memories of people she had never heard of facts which could be processed in her own mind and then emerge as convincing little dramatic episodes. How could she have known about the President's gruel? How could she have become aware of the surname Boettiger? Did she fish or was she told? The former seems as unlikely as sitting with a rod at the end of Brighton pier and catching a fish which one particular person several thousand miles away had marked beforehand.

Almost as strange as the disclosure of evidential detail is the way in which the communicator, who had deliberately taken the initiative in the first and third sessions, became cautious and wary in the fifth. This was quite in keeping with her character as the secretary of an important political person. If Geraldine had been fishing for clues with her wide-ranging mind, one would have supposed she might have found some, to make her impersonation stronger.

The second sequence of scripts concerned someone who had lived even further away from Britain during his lifetime, and of whom Geraldine had never heard. Ambrose Pratt had been an Australian, the son of an English father who had emigrated after qualifying as a doctor and set up a practice in New South Wales. Ambrose trained as a lawyer but then went over into journalism and authorship. His interests were wide, embracing left-wing politics, zoology and eastern religious thought among other matters. He wrote fiction which found a considerable number of readers.

His friends found him a fascinating conversationalist. He developed a certain measure of psychic awareness; he could see, so it appeared, people's auras, which enabled him to understand their bodily and mental states, so that he knew what or what not to say, and how or how not to say it.

During sleep he indulged in what is sometimes termed astral travelling. He himself called it 'going out', and what he could remember of such occasions he wrote down in journals. He died at the age of seventy in 1944.

For the last ten years of his life he was a close friend of the Australian scientist Raynor Johnson. The latter wrote of him as follows:

> Ambrose passed over at the age of seventy to a world with which in some measure he was already familiar. Few men of his generation can have had a greater variety of experience or touched more sides of life with distinction. He had explored the inner worlds as far as he was permitted to go. He had travelled in many different parts of the world and done adventurous things. He had taken an active part in politics behind the scenes, he had been a journalist and editor, an economist and a successful writer of imaginative books. He possessed marked artistic gifts if he had cared to concentrate upon them, but he set them aside. He was a mystic at heart, but this interest he kept secret except from a friend or two. He moved with great ease and friendliness among other men, but always there was a subtle air of distinction in his personality which others freely recognised ... He moved through ordinary life with an inward confidence in his power to meet whatever it brought to him.[2]

Johnson, who had a deep interest in psychical research, first became aware of Geraldine Cummins and her gifts when he read the two 'Myers' books which she had produced, which have been described above in Chapter Seven. In 1953, when he was in London, he paid a call on her, and as he was about to leave he remarked that he had never had any first hand communication with a discarnate person. She replied by suggesting that he left with her some handwriting to facilitate a link, which he did. The following month, after he had returned to Australia,

---

[2] *The Decisive Testimony*, page 54.

TWO EVIDENTIALLY-IMPRESSIVE SCRIPT SEQUENCES

he received a letter from her containing some script. She had herself not been very impressed by it and felt that it might well be 'all nonsense'. It referred to a man who 'when on earth had a higher nature that gave him supreme moments of understanding', and who was

> ... some kind of official. He administrated. The work to earn his daily bread was of no interest to him. What mattered was his secret life ... He died during the war, some time in the middle of it. But he was not in it. He worked and lived in Australia. I see him in a big town with a very fine beautiful harbour. I must try to get his name. He shows me the letters Electron. He says it is a foreign word. It is Greek and means Amber. Now he shows me a rose. I see what he means; his name is Amber Rose. He makes a little fish, a sprat. Amberose Prat. He cuts off the sign of S. He makes it clear his name was Amberose Pratt. He says the writer of this letter you hold was a friend of his.[3]

The letter impressed Johnson, but he wondered if he had mentioned Pratt's name to Geraldine in the course of conversation. Queried about it, she thought he had not. In regard to that, one may remark that if the whole name had been installed somewhere in her memory it was rather strange that it came through allusively in the same way as Marguerite Le Hand's had done. All the other facts given were correct. So the script was indicative of ESP, but not of more than telepathy between the living, since all the facts were already known to the enquirer.

Johnson wrote back in January 1954 thanking her for the script, which he assured her was by no means nonsense, and asked her to obtain, if she could, replies from Pratt to a few personal questions. Two months later he received a second script, not now in Astor's characteristic writing but in another hand (though it was not recognisably Pratt's) in which the personal questions were answered briefly; the bulk of it, however, constituted what was in effect a letter from Pratt to Johnson, and contained some quite unexpected material. It referred to a book Johnson had written, *The Imprisoned Splendour*, said that a group of discarnate spirits had given him the ideas it contained, and specifically asked him to study the philosophic writings of Douglas Fawcett[4] which had already come to his attention before he proceeded

---

[3] *The Decisive Testimony*, page 58.
[4] A younger brother of the Colonel Fawcett who disappeared in Brazil - see Chapter 8 above.

with another book, since in the view of the group Fawcett's philosophy of Imagism' was

> ... a new and original outlook on the Cosmos, based on metaphysical argument, sound and straightforward and to a great extent intelligible to the reader not trained in philosophy ... On the main and essential points, I, a traveller in eternity, who has had further and amazing mystical experiences since leaving earth, can assure you of the Tightness of Fawcett's views.
>
> He demonstrates how useless are such concepts as that of the Absolute. He reconciles man's own innate sense of the freedom of the will with a Cosmos that is not so determinate in character as Science would have it. He has provided a satisfactory solution of the riddle of Evil, and clarified ideas on Time. Above all, in constructive thought he excels.[5]

This reference to Fawcett was something Johnson had by no means expected. He had been in touch with Fawcett, who had sent him an appreciative note on *The Imprisoned Splendour* together with a publisher's leaflet advertising his own two books, *The Zermatt Dialogues* and *The Oberland Dialogues*, which he thought might interest Johnson. This was something that Geraldine had not known, though she did know of the two books since she had reviewed them for a magazine; she had also visited Douglas Fawcett and his wife and had tea with them. So, on the whole, the second script, so far as concerned content, could be explained by what was already in her own mind, with perhaps some assistance from telepathy from the living. However, it was the style which impressed Johnson, and the fact that the script referred to an event which few people, perhaps only three, knew - the fact that Fawcett had been in touch with Johnson. (Though, of course, Geraldine might have picked this up by telepathy from Johnson, unimportant though it was to the latter at the time.)

The would-be believer and the doubting Thomas within the latter now began to contend. Ambrose Pratt, if it were he, had urged him to study Fawcett's books and then himself write a new book based to some extent on Fawcett's insights.

The former he might easily do; the latter would be a considerable

---

[5] *The Decisive Testimony*, pages 61-62.

TWO EVIDENTIALLY-IMPRESSIVE SCRIPT SEQUENCES

undertaking. He decided to attempt to obtain an independent reference to the matter through another medium, and wrote to Geraldine as follows:

> Now if only my friend Ambrose would find a sensitive, not known to you, not known to Douglas Fawcett and not known to me, and instruct this sensitive to send to Johnson, Queen's College, Melbourne, even one significant sentence, this would be a satisfactory proof of the origin of the script.[6]

He also asked her to read aloud for Ambrose Pratt's benefit a letter to him in which he said he accepted the task which the group had asked him to perform, and added a number of questions.

The script which he received eight weeks later suggested that Johnson should have already received reassurance of identification from the material given in the previous scripts,[7] and reinforced the request to write the new book.

Johnson accordingly wrote again to Geraldine for Pratt's benefit, saying he would like the last doubt in his mind removed, and that if his friend would take the initiative and find another medium through whom to send a significant sentence, this would suffice. The reply was as follows:

> It is good to have this letter from you and to feel your nearness in every line of the writing... Only you and an order from my Group-soul could bring me back to what is now to me like an underground region in which, like a worm blindly grubbing in the earth, I sought you and found you. But I could not have found you if there had not been what I might call a vibratory light. You met this sensitive, and then Ambrose was no longer the worm, he became a glow-worm...

> You write of a last 10% of doubt which you demand should be removed. From my point of view I should be doing you a wrong to remove it. Should there not be a ten per cent of faith in your composition?... I take it the reply is in the negative, so I am prepared to be the blindworm grubbing further in the clay of earth, but on certain conditions. There

---

[6] *The Decisive Testimony*, page 65.
[7] The trouble was that telepathy between Johnson and Geraldine could not be absolutely excluded.

has to be a something to light the lamp of the worm... The sensitive in question has to be on a high vibratory measure.. Convey through a second party some object that I possessed when on earth - even a few lines of my handwriting... The second... should give the object to a stranger, who takes it to the sensitive; then, God willing, I may get the message through to you which is your wish.

He went on to explain his present discarnate interests, ending with a statement that would intrigue and perhaps raise the eyebrows of a theologian.

Bear in mind above all that God is living, not finished - a static pillar of salt like Lot's wife. He is first and last a Creator, therefore He is creative of Himself, adding to His measure and to eventual bliss all the little souls. Dismiss from your mind the idea of a Spiritual Absolute.[8]

Johnson's reaction was to feel that the 'competent, critical and authoritative' quality of the scripts he had so far received was a sufficient guarantee to him of their genuineness, so he decided after all not to seek a second opinion from another medium in the way indicated to him, and got on with the writing of the new book. He continued to receive scripts from this source until July 1960, when Geraldine told him she thought she should not write any more for him as circumstances were obliging her to curtail her psychic work.

As to these further scripts he remarks:

The procedure was as indicated before. I would write a letter to my friend Ambrose and send it to Miss Cummins. She would read this before trying for further script... I do not regard these scripts as 'verbal inspiration'. I regard the subconscious mind of the sensitive as telepathically receptive of the ideas of Ambrose Pratt, but providing to some degree the language expressing them. At the same time I am bound to say that particularly in one script ... he has managed to reproduce the lyrical and exciting quality of his own style.[9]

It is perhaps worth quoting a passage from the last script received, in January 1960.

---

[8] *The Decisive Testimony*, page 68.
[9] *The Decisive Testimony*, pages 70-71.

TWO EVIDENTIALLY-IMPRESSIVE SCRIPT SEQUENCES

For reasons created by his past lives anterior to this earth life, a man has unconsciously created the design, generally speaking, of his Fate during his present earthly existence. The kind of temptations, difficulties, etc., are in the big events already there before him. Will he overcome them or will he fail? He has free will, the power to choose. But Raynor, my dear fellow, if you had it your way you would load the dice ... In order to make progress, in order that his self may grow, the religious man or mystic has to struggle, suffer pain, perhaps lose faith, perhaps, oh horror, be lost in the Dark Night of the Soul. There can be no short cuts for him. While he is on earth a certain limitation has to be his lot.

Incidentally I may remind you that when on the Cross Christ the Son of God cried out, 'My God, my God, why has Thou forsaken me?' Why did God the loving Father permit his Son to be driven to the depths of such despair? Why in that awful hour did He not buoy Christ up, preserve his lost faith, by holding before him the vision of his glorious resurrection? Would it not have carried him through in a state of wonder, thanksgiving and inspiration - made it all easy? Yes, but then the Crucifixion would not have been the supreme test it was, a test that through the centuries since has shown the Christian how the Son of Man failed, and yet the God within that Son of Man eventually succeeded despite that despairing cry.[10]

This sequence of scripts, resembling as they did the sort of personal letters which he might have expected to receive from his friend had he still been alive on earth, convinced Johnson that Ambrose Pratt was the real originator, even though the sort of evidence needed to convince a conscientious psychical researcher was lacking. Making allowance for the fact of their being mediated through another person's mental processes, they still seemed authentic because of the things they said. Sir Oliver Lodge, as we have seen, reacted in a similar way to the 'Myers' scripts he was shown. It was rather as if a breeze from the open sea were passing through a dense forest of pine trees before reaching human nostrils.

What might be scented in the first few breaths would be the odours proper to pines, but then one might detect the salt sea air and ozone as well. This is no doubt what it has to be, a mixture, partly of what is earthy, but also *Murmurs and scents of the infinite sea.*

---

[10] *The Decisive Testimony*, page 91.

11

INDIRECT PSYCHIATRY

Over some twenty years, from the middle thirties to the middle fifties of this century, Geraldine engaged in an unusual partnership with her brother, Dr Robert Cummins, a physician who practised in Ireland. Whatever may be thought of her other psychic work, there can be no question that this association was beneficial to those on whose behalf it operated, since it resulted in healings from mental illnesses and from physical symptoms which accompanied them. If miracles attributed to saints, whether biblical or extra-biblical, are to be counted as signs that God was with them, one cannot, if one is any sort of theist, refuse to consider that what the two of them did together should be similarly regarded. As Jesus remarked, in reference to his own healings, how can Satan cast out Satan?

Among her psychic powers Geraldine possessed that of psychometry, the ability accurately to state things about the owner of an object which is being handled. How this happens is a completely mystery; *that* it happens would be generally agreed among psychical researchers. Many mediums, having this gift, use it to latch on' to a person, living or departed, who once owned the article they are given to handle. In Geraldine's case, however, the consequence was very much more than accurate statements about the living or the recently dead. She could, so she believed, obtain a whole family history, stretching back many years; not merely the tree but its roots came into view. From what was disclosed in her automatic writing about the past lives of a person's ancestors, features of that person's present life could be explained. Robert Cummins, when observing in some of his patients symptoms which did not respond to the customary medical or psychiatric treatments, sometimes referred the matter to his sister. He did not of course disclose the patient's medical history (which would have been a breach of professional confidence) but would with the patient's agreement borrow an object from the latter and enclose it in a letter to Geraldine, asking her what associations it evoked.

The reply, copied from an automatically-written script (which might be of considerable length), having been received, was imparted in part or whole to the patient. In almost every case the latter, understanding that his disability was linked either to an early traumatic experience of his own or else to a similarly unfortunate ancestral experience, was able to overcome his difficulty; the symptom or symptoms passed away and he was able to lead a normal life.

In 1957 the two of them published a selection of these cases in a book, *Healing the Mind*. The authors are named as 'R. Connell' and Geraldine Cummins; medical ethics required him to refrain from advertising himself, but no such anonymity was required of his sister, and no doubt many guessed who was the other partner in the enterprise. Dr Cummins wrote an introduction to the book, parts of which are now quoted:

> The small group of Medical cases whose histories are recorded in the following series are published in order to illustrate a method of investigation and treatment of psychological disorders that has not yet been applied systematically ... so far as the writer is aware. The method concerns the deliberate employment of extrasensory perception.
>
> The method was first employed in the case of a businessman, who was faced with the prospect of loss of occupation and ruin, and whose life was threatened by intermittent attacks of acute alcoholic poisoning...
>
> After each attack he remained cured for a varying period, and an abstainer. Each recovery was succeeded by a disheartening relapse of his malady. After the last attack ... he confessed that on certain occasions ... he found himself quite unable to sign his own name ... Alcohol enabled him to overcome the inhibition, and for this reason he took it. His father, he stated, had suffered from the same writing inhibition.

It was inferred that if the cause of the writing inhibition could be discovered and explained to the patient, it might be possible to remove it, and with it the periodic alcoholism. It was thought... that it would be both time-consuming and difficult to determine the cause by any of the methods of investigation in use at that time...

The patient appeared to be suffering from an inherited psychosis whose roots extended back into the past. It had not been uncovered by two specialists. It was decided by the writer to endeavour to discover the cause of the neurosis by utilising the faculty of ESP... The manner in which this investigation was carried out is recorded in a subsequent chapter. The dramatic and unexpected success which ensued led to the application of ESP in other obscure psychological disorders...

over a period of twenty years...

It is suggested that the history of these selected cases is adequate evidence of the value of this method of investigation, when employed judiciously, in psychological disturbances of an obscure nature...

The family physician has not been engaged in proving any scientific hypothesis in regard to ESP... The object has been to cure or relieve his patients. Exact scientific observation and proofs of the sensitive's findings have not been pursued beyond the needs of the case in consequence, and any deductions therefore made are limited.[1]

Twenty cases are cited in the book, some described at length, others more briefly. To cover them all would extend this chapter unduly, so three are summarised, each referring to a different type of malady.

The first, the one mentioned by Dr Cummins in his introduction, concerned a professional man aged 46, who after a period of strain in his personal life took to drink and was eventually found to be suffering from *delirium tremens*.

After treatment in an institution he was discharged, apparently cured of his alcoholism, but two years later began to suffer acute attacks of stomach pains, the last of which responded to treatment only with difficulty. He had in fact been reverting to alcohol - yet seemed able, after each attack, to give it up without difficulty. When asked why,

---

[1] *Healing the Mind*, pages 7-9.

in that case, he did not give it up permanently, he replied that he had a peculiar inhibition; when, on occasions of importance, he had to sign his name, he found he could not do so.

This was specially the case when he had to sign cheques. His father, in his later years, had suffered from the same inhibition. A dose of alcohol removed it; hence the continual reversion.

The first attempt to overcome the mental blockage was made through auto-suggestion. He was told that some racial inheritance was the reason for his strange inability; this was suggested because his father had similarly suffered. Some catastrophe had occurred to an ancestor. He was asked, whenever he knew he had cheques to sign, to suggest to himself the previous day that the cause of his inability was a thing of the past and had nothing to do with his own conscious mind. The suggested method worked - but of course it was an *ad hoc*, temporary method which did not get at the root of the trouble. It was desirable to remove the blockage altogether. Psychiatric assistance was considered, but as he had twice been treated by psychiatrists while in a home for inebriates it was decided that a new approach was needed. (Though Dr Cummins does not say so, it seems likely that his knowledge of his sister's gifts suggested this new approach.) An old family document in the patient's possession was sent to Geraldine, who used it to 'home in' on the patient and his family history.

The consequence was a lengthy account of misfortunes alleged to have been experienced by the patient's ancestors, going back to the thirteenth century. Two fears, it was said, underlay his inhibition. Some of his ancestors had been Jews. They had, when living in Venice, been obliged to leave a palace they had owned and live in a ghetto with other Jews. They lost their wealth and for a while were in abject poverty. Eventually they travelled to Spain and tried to live there obscurely while maintaining the practice of their Jewish faith. For a while they managed to evade the notice of the Inquisition and their fortunes improved. Then one of their number, a certain Juan Davila, renounced his faith to marry a Spanish noblewoman, and was cursed by his father for doing so. Letters between the two families fell into the hands of the Spanish authorities and every member of Juan's family was seized. Some died in prison, some were burned, some were tortured. Juan, one of the latter, was broken on the wheel in his wife's presence. He regarded the tragedy his family had suffered as due to her because of what she had written in her letters, and his last words to her were of bitter hatred. She herself went insane, and Juan's posthumous son was born while she was still in this state.

She recovered, lived with her father's family for a while, but was then suspected of having herself become a Jewess.

To get her out of the way and prevent embarrassment for her family she was sent to England, where she adopted a new surname and lived with an English relation. She had developed an abhorrence of writing, since this had been the cause of her husband's downfall and that of his family. The son born to her was taught to read and write, but it was necessary to keep his mother from ever witnessing this.

Helped by money from his relatives in Spain, he became a successful merchant, but the fear that his mother passed on to him was such that he often found it impossible to write his own name.

'This story contains the roots of this conflict. Such a psychological trait as this fear may be carried on . . . for centuries.'

The document obtained by Geraldine was read to the patient, and he was told how it had been produced. A second statement, obtained somewhat later, urged that he be told the 'hidden history' of his family. 'The reason he cannot write at times is due to the letters written by an ancestor who betrayed her husband and his family. Added to that is another fear. This man respected and loved his father. When he learned of his father's incapacity at times to write his name it came as a shock to his mind. It roused the dormant race-fear, which came to control him at intervals.' This second statement, too, was read to the patient.

Somewhat later yet a third statement was obtained, describing a family tragedy occurring to one of the patient's ancestors (subsequent to the happenings in Spain) which revived the old fears and made them continue.

Having had all the above related to him (much abbreviated in this account) the patient recovered completely from the writing inhibition, overcame his addiction to alcohol and later became Chairman of the Company to which he belonged.

The second case, a much shorter one, was that of a young woman in her early twenties who worked as an assistant in a chemist's shop and who began to experience fits of dizziness which came upon her suddenly, both indoors and out of doors. Neither a holiday nor a course of treatment with appropriate drugs improved her condition. Eventually she had to give up her work. There appeared to be no physical reason for her attacks. A specimen of her handwriting was sent to Geraldine, who obtained some script on the matter.

In this instance no lengthy history, ancestral or racial, was given; instead physical and psychological reasons were adduced. Parts of the script are quoted below:

I feel in this handwriting a young and very sensitive girl...rather run down, just a little below par ... a centre of balance in her brain does not always function absolutely instantaneously with the mind. This would not affect her balance (so very slight in this weakness) if it were not that her nervous system is easily stimulated by her subconscious mind.

The subconscious ... has conveyed this self-preservation fear with some force to the consciousness, which indeed is now haunted by what is really an unreasoning fear ... The girl is neither neurotic nor hysterical and her brain is perfectly normal.

All that is actually physically wrong is a slightly slow functioning of the centre of balance just about the time of the (monthly) period. She ought at that time to take things fairly easily for a day or two. She should also lead for a time a healthy outdoor life and try to take plenty of exercise and fresh air.

I recommend a special form of exercise she could do [the nature of the exercise is then specified] ... She should be told there is no trouble in her brain to cause her to be afraid ... She has actually a quite sufficient sense of balance to keep her walking and running in an erect position without difficulty.

There was an added cause in her being in the chemist's place of business for a short time ... The enclosed place roused the dormant fear which is allied to claustrophobia in this particular symptom.

I think the patient should not be given a sedative but ... be stimulated by a good tonic. It is necessary to make her physically as well and strong as possible ... She is definitely a normal and intelligent person and can herself overcome the terror if she can relax completely and say aloud to herself that owing to better health she has nothing to fear any more...[2]

The consequence of having the report read to her was that the young woman returned to work, continued at it and was herself satisfied that she had fully recovered.

---

[2] *Healing the Mind*, pages 44-46.

The third case mentioned here was of a twenty-two years' old medical student who suffered from asthma, though there was no history of this disease in his family. When he was sixteen he was treated for catarrh, and the injections he had been given provoked a condition in which he was almost unable to breathe. He took adrenalin to afford some relief, and found he had continually to inject himself with it, especially when he faced examinations; it was even necessary to inject himself during the examinations themselves. In general the attacks were worse at night than during the daytime. When he first came to get medical treatment it was observed that his arms were pitted with puncture marks. A special vaccine was prepared from swabs from his nose and throat, but three months' administration of it had no beneficial effect. Eventually a course of peptone injections led to a great improvement, and for six months the doctor saw no more of him, until one day he brought his mother for consultation.

She was a school teacher, aged fifty-nine, who had a high blood pressure, was very much overweight and suffered from violent headaches. Treatment was prescribed, but before it could take effect she became unconscious and remained so for three days. A cerebral oedema was diagnosed. Despite all that could be done for her she got worse and worse, and died a few months later. Her illness had an immediate effect on her son; as soon as she suffered her first lapse into unconsciousness his asthma returned, and no treatment, including that previously successful with peptones, was of any avail. It was thought that his condition might be aggravated by a nervous complex. So recourse was had to Geraldine. His fountain pen was sent to her, and with this as a link she got quite a quantity of script. Again, no reference was made to any ancestral situations. The cause, it was said, had occurred when he was badly frightened during an illness.

> There is a strong energy between him and his mother ... I see that when he was very young ... he had an illness in which he was gravely frightened. I think he has no memory of that illness ...

> There was feverishness and it was connected with some difficulty in breathing. His mother was looking after him then and was the all-important figure in his life.

> Trust seems betrayed to a small child when . . . the mother fails to shelter the baby from terror. The small child then has an unreasoning

feeling of desertion and helplessness ... This complex of temporary helplessness was created in the subconscious mind of the little child by the illness-terror connected with the difficulty in breathing. In later life it would therefore be likely to be associated with the apparatus of breathing ...

[The illness-terror] lay dormant in his unconscious mind [but was] roused to life by some very mistaken treatment, an overdose of something given him when he first had asthma. It was ... analogous to that brief but terrifying condition when he was a baby ...

The old, unreasoning, infantile terror is now active, and the cause of these nervous spasms. The terror received a double vitality from the shock of the mother's sudden illness. The mother's brief unconsciousness produced anticipation of her death ... Although the mother recovered temporarily the harm was done - the old infantile terror given an artificial life He must realise that these nervous spasms are produced by a purely irrational terror ... Knowing now what it is, from henceforth he will have no difficulty in breathing. The physical cause of his illness has been removed by the recent treatment ... He will be entirely free from asthma when he faces his examiners, once he has definitely grasped and accepted the fundamental cause of his asthmatic condition.[3]

Once the report had been read to and explained to the patient, the psychological factor being emphasised, the attacks subsided at once, despite the fact that the mother was manifestly getting worse. The peptone injections were discontinued but the cure was evidently permanent.

These three abbreviated case-histories are generally representative of the others described in the book, and provoke a number of reflections. We are of course not here necessarily dealing with a purported discarnate agency which provided the information and advice. It may have been so; Geraldine may have thought so, and so may her brother, but no such claim is made. The book merely says the information was obtained 'through ESP'. The essential feature in each case was that a disturbed mental state was relieved through an explanatory story, which somehow loosened the log-jam within the mind and allowed normal living to recommence. Satisfying assurances preceded complete cures.

---

[3] *Healing the Mind*, pages 58-60.

One is reminded of the story in the Gospels in which a paralysed man is first assured by Jesus that his sins are forgiven, and then is told to pick up his bed and walk away.

Psycho-analysis, in its more probing and expensive manner, does something like this too, though it does not claim to reach back beyond a person's infancy.

What Geraldine displayed, therefore, was insight, either her own or that of some unknown entity which directed her hand. The cases do seem to be evidential of ESP, since she correctly read, from the object she held, the conditions and backgrounds of the patients. One does not however need to suggest more than telepathy between the living, between herself and her brother.

One wonders whether Dr Cummins' method of facilitating cures by obtaining ESP readings, as reported in this small book which probably did not have many readers, may have inspired other general practitioners to do the same. He was fortunate in having a highly talented sensitive at hand with whom he could work in complete confidence because she was his sister and they trusted one another. This would be a rare state of affairs. He might, of course, have sought a wider audience among his professional colleagues by submitting these cases in his own name to a recognised medical journal. However, that would have been at the cost of his reputation. That the method worked successfully would not in itself have impressed any doctor. After all, placebos work. Then, even more than now, anything psychic was disreputable. To suggest that there might be something in it was like a soldier in trench warfare imprudently putting his head above the parapet and inviting the attentions of a sniper. It was safest to remain in the well-worn groove. Dr Cummins showed his head briefly, but wearing the tin hat of anonymity, and was content to be a voice crying, not too loudly, in the wilderness.

12

THE COOMBE TENNANT SCRIPTS

During the period, now somewhat more than a century, when psychical research has been actively pursued by people concerned to apply scientific methods of enquiry and rigid canons of evidence, every so often something quite remarkable has shown up, which cannot be explained away as a consequence of fraud, mal-observation, misunderstanding or chance coincidence. Sometimes the facts, while utterly anomalous, do not seem to suggest anything important or humanly significant; one may instance the levitations of D.D. Home and others, or the sometimes well-attested materialisation phenomena. At other times they do seem to suggest that the assumptions we generally make, in particular about non-survival of bodily death, are at fault. The mind boggles at the idea of conscious awareness being independent of the nervous system with which it is associated, and continuing in a life of its own after the brain has decomposed, but when messages are received through sensitives which would be regarded as amply demonstrative of continued conscious existence if they came from a living person, and if they occur over and over again, giving verifiable facts and coming across in that person's characteristic style, one has to ask if the boggling is perhaps more a reflex action than a sensible response, knee-jerk instead of knowledge, and whether Hamlet was perfectly right in saying that there are more things in heaven and earth than are dreamt of in our philosophy. Such occurrences are rare, like prominent peaks in a long mountain range. It was given to

Geraldine Cummins, towards the end of her life, to produce one of the most impressive of these summits, perhaps the most impressive piece of evidence for survival of death so far to be documented. It may have been as striking as it was because the communicator purported to be someone who in her earthly lifetime had been a gifted psychic of considerable repute, though she carefully preserved her anonymity and only a very few persons knew she was psychically sensitive at all. The sequence of scripts in question, together with an introduction by Professor C. D. Broad of Cambridge University, and comments by Geraldine herself and one of her friends, has been published and deserves to be read in full and with care, not only because of its evidential features but on account of its intrinsic interest.

It is not in the slightest degree like anything Geraldine wrote at any other time, whether of herself or under the influence of some controlling entity. It reads like what it purports to be, a rather rambling series of memoirs written from beyond the grave.[1]

Mrs Winifred Margaret Coombe Tennant, born in Gloucestershire in 1874, the daughter of a naval officer George Pearce Serocold and his second wife, both of them Welsh, married Charles Coombe Tennant, a man just over twice her age and a member of a distinguished Glamorgan family, in 1895. She thus became the sister-in-law of Frederic Myers, who had married her husband's sister Eveleen fifteen years earlier, and through him came to know some of the foundation members of the Society for Psychical Research; Myers in particular she respected and admired, though she disliked his wife. She had altogether four children; her eldest son, Christopher, was killed in action in Flanders when not quite twenty; her only daughter died in infancy in 1908; subsequently she had two sons, Alexander and Henry, born in 1909 and 1913. Her husband died in 1928. She made her home at the Coombe Tennants' family residence at Cadoxton Lodge, north of Swansea, and lived a full life for a woman of her class and period, being a firm adherent of the Liberal Party, a supporter of Women's Suffrage and Welsh Nationalism, an active participant in local affairs, and also for many years a magistrate. She was very well-read, and took a special interest in Art, making for herself a valuable collection of pictures by modern French artists. She had a decided and forceful personality and could at times be combative. No one who knew her could, and no one did, associate her with anything psychic.

---

[1] See *Swan on a Black Sea*, Geraldine Cummins. Routledge & Kegan Paul, 1965 and Pelegrin Trust with Pilgrim Books, 1986.

It was not until after her baby daughter Daphne had died that she began to take an interest in psychical matters, when she began to feel herself to be in touch with the spirits of some of the 'old guard' of the Society for Psychical Research, particularly Frederic Myers, who had died seven years earlier and to whom she was of course related. Her mediumship extended from 1908, when she began to get automatic script which claimed to be from Myers. It was then modified three times; first 'Myers' asked her not to try to write automatically but to endeavour to grasp ideas which he would seek to convey to her mentally, and to write them down; next both 'Myers' and 'Gurney'[2] asked her to sit in the presence of Sir Oliver Lodge and dictate her impressions to him; finally she was asked to confine her sittings to occasions when Gerald Balfour[3] could be present and act as note-taker, since he as a philosopher would be interested in the process of communication as well as in what was produced. From 1911 until 1931 Gerald Balfour was her only sitter. A very large number of sessions took place, either at her home in Wales or at his at Fisher Hill, Woking. In this way she became closely attached to Balfour and his wife and got to know his sister, Eleanor, one of the most intelligent and intellectual women of her day, who had married Henry Sidgwick, the first President of the Society for Psychical Research.

During this time she produced much of the material which, taken together with the productions of other automatists, constituted the famous 'Cross-Correspondences'[4] which extended from 1906 over some twenty years. At the same time her psychic abilities were known only to herself and the few who collaborated with her, and the secret was carefully kept. Whenever reference was made to her in print it was always under her chosen pseudonym, 'Mrs Willett'. Not until after her death was it made known who she really was.

One of those who did know that Mrs Coombe Tennant and 'Mrs Willett' were one and the same was the then Secretary of the Society

---

[2] Edmund Gurney (1847-1888), a founder-member of the SPR.

[3] Gerald Balfour (1853-1945), brother of A. J. Balfour (Conservative Prime Minister 1902-1905) and a distinguished philosopher and psychical researcher.

[4] After a number of the founder-members of the SPR had died a number of sensitives associated with that body began to receive fragments of material, usually references to classical or other literary works, sometimes very obscure, which meant nothing singly but when pieced together made meaningful allusions to passages which the deceased founders would have known and appreciated. It increasingly appeared that an experiment initiated 'from the other side' was being carried out to convince undeceased colleagues of the continued existences of their former associates as active intelligences.

for Psychical Research, W. H. Salter, whose wife was Helen Verrall, herself the daughter of Professor A. W. Verrall and his wife Margaret Verrall, both classical scholars and members of the SPR. Professor Verrall purported to be one of the discarnate group engaged in transmitting the 'Cross-Correspondence' material; his wife and daughter were both among the automatist recipients of that material. A year after Mrs Coombe Tennant's death Salter, in August 1957, wrote to Geraldine, who was then on holiday in County Cork, to ask if she would take part in an attempt to contact the deceased mother (i.e. Mrs Coombe Tennant) of a member of the SPR, who wanted to give her the opportunity of sending him a message. Salter indicated that he thought the case would interest Geraldine, since the circumstances 'were peculiar'.

Geraldine agreed, and was sent the name of the enquirer, Major Coombe Tennant, which meant nothing at all to her, and a query whether she would wish to have specimens of the deceased lady's handwriting to facilitate contact. Geraldine agreed to this also, but decided that she would first try for script unaided by her natural gift for psychometry. The first three scripts were written at her home in Woodville, Glanmire. She had no clue at all as to who the expected communicator might be. She also could not know at the time just how genuinely evidential her writing was. In fact, in the course of these scripts, amounting in all to about 2,400 words, some thirty accurate specific statements appear, and no provably inaccurate ones. It was rather like someone playing darts blindfold and hitting the bull's eye each time.

The first script, though making correct references to the communicator, came entirely from the control, Astor. In the second the communicator contributed two short paragraphs towards the end. In the third she predominated, as in all subsequent scripts, and brought a characteristic style, which remained throughout. A short quotation may serve to show what it was like.

From the fourth script: September 22nd 1957

Dear G.C.

Listen - please listen - Ah! the word leaps up to me. It is Morgan. Hold on to Morgan. Now there is a famous cricketer, W. G. Grace. Cut off Grace. It's W. G. I want. If you add on W. G. to Morgan you have a name that may not appear to make sense, but it does make sense to me. I spent many happy years of my life, loving, living in Morganwg. My mother, too, came from there. This has to do with the origin of the species. My husband and my species or race. The most important events in my life took place in Morganwg. I mean those that relate to origins, the birth of what we are, the mould of our creation as regards influences. I found my husband in Morganwg.[5] By the time the fifth script had been written Geraldine was beginning to suspect the identity of the communicator. The third script had said she had been an automatist during her life on earth; in the fifth she was introduced as 'Mrs Wills'.

This caused Geraldine to think that she might be in touch with the 'Mrs Willett' whose mediumship was known to all the Psychical Research cognoscenti. She herself had recently met a Mrs Wills when visiting a friend west of Cork and it seemed likely to her that the latter had, so to speak, blocked the former. In the sixth script the statement was made: 'I am Mrs Wills. That is not quite right. Never mind, press on.' From then on she was convinced that her guess had been correct, and realised why Salter had thought the case would interest her because the circumstances were peculiar. However, she still knew no more about the communicator's real identity than the latter chose to tell her in the scripts, beyond the fact of her surname, which could be inferred from the name of her son.

Once the sixth script had been written she temporarily gave up the attempt to get more. She had already sent to Major Coombe Tennant through Salter plenty of material in response to his request - some 7,000 words, in fact. After she had returned to London in October 1957 the latter called on her and asked if she would be willing to try to obtain more scripts. At the time she declined because she knew she was going to have many other things to do during the winter.

Salter must have been disappointed because in the sixth script there was some deeply interesting material referring to the domestic life of Myers and to the fate of his eldest son, who had committed suicide. As Myers himself was not mentioned in the script by name, Geraldine almost certainly would not have known what situations were being referred to - unless super-ESP was making one of its alleged prodigious efforts - but Salter will have recognised the allusions and naturally would have wanted to hear more from this remarkably accurate source.

However, her refusal was not her last word on the subject.

Her interest seems to have been re-stimulated after reading in January 1958 an obituary of Mrs Coombe Tennant in the Journal of the SPR.

---

[5] *Swan on a Black Sea*, page 17.

A month later the sequence was recommenced. Once launched into it, she found the personality of the communicator so attractive (despite occasional acerbities) that she continued to try for scripts at irregular intervals - from February 14th-20th one each day, and thereafter at irregular intervals over a period of six months. Subsequently the intervals became longer, and the last script was written at the end of November 1959. Not until this had been written did she meet Mrs Coombe Tennant's two sons, who had by then seen all the communications and found them impressive, both as to content, which was almost always correct, and as to style, which often seemed entirely characteristic of their mother. There was, however, a final script written three and a half months later still, which appeared unexpectedly when Geraldine was giving a sitting to a member of the SPR; Mrs Coombe Tennant (if it was she) intruded, brought in Helen Salter (who had died a year earlier) and the latter gave her husband two messages.

Most of the whole sequence of communications were purported reminiscences of Mrs Coombe Tennant's earthly life. Some contained personal advice for her sons (one script was too personal to be published) and quite a few touched on her work as the sensitive, 'Mrs Willett'. To summarise the contents would extend this chapter too greatly; the book is essential reading for anyone interested in parapsychology, and short cuts are no substitute. A couple of extracts may be offered, however, because of their general interest. One, in script number 7, referred to the Conservative statesman A.J. Balfour in his old age, and referred to a romance of his youth, known to a few but not to the world at large until it was revealed by Jean Balfour in an article in the *Journal* of the SPR in February 1960 just two years later than the script, which appropriately was written on St Valentine's Day. The communicator is reminiscing.

> Many years ago I spent a strange hour in a room being one of a trio. We were listening to great music. All was peaceful. But the music did not carry me away. It peopled the room with the invisible dead. But at first I felt rather than perceived their presences. As I now know I became linked with the third in the trio, the deeper mind of a living man, who was resting and relaxed and appeared to be half asleep. And suddenly the presences of the dead I sensed became one visible presence from another life. I saw nothing ghostly. It was as real to me as my hand - simply a woman wearing an old-fashioned costume. She was of another period. But I want you to realise that it was the third

of the trio - this old man of eighty years of so - who gave me the power in some curious way to see this young woman, so attractive, the embodiment of youth, who literally shone down upon him as she stood beside him - rays of a hidden sun, as it were, emanating from her body as she stood looking down at him.

To me the effect was utterly strange, non-human, yet in appearance she was wholly human, with hair thick and beautiful.

In that period women cherished their long hair, of course, she was so dated by that dress she wore. But the old man was old enough to be her grandfather, yet he was her contemporary, and I felt from this illumination she cast upon him she loved him not as one loves a grandfather, but as a woman loves a man greatly of her own generation. He so ancient and she so young, yet they had been young once together. There's a riddle for you! But I later learnt that I had seen and described to my companion, the second in the trio, one dead many years. That this vision of mine meant much to this old man who was lying down resting, oblivious of this visitor. She was of his early manhood, and there had been no other in his long life! Incredible, you will say! But when I met him he was cold and austere, and I was in awe of his admirable intellect. He had schooled himself, punished himself, like a flagellating saint, and so had kept himself immaculate for her.

That scene I have described took its toll of me. As she you will call the ghost appeared beside the aged man, I felt myself slipping fading, passing into the sleep of trance. Oh! I was always afraid of losing control, of being banished. It meant I might unfit myself for my work in life, which was dear to me. So I struggled frantically to keep hold on myself. I got back, but that meant the ghost disappeared.[6]

This episode, featuring Mrs Coombe Tennant when she was already fifty-five, widowed, and a considerable public figure in her home county (hence her unwillingness to be liable to fall into trances) is mentioned in Gerald Balfour's *Study of the Psychological Aspects of Mrs. Willett's Mediumship* which formed Volume 43 of the Proceedings of the SPR issued in 1935. His account, however, did not suggest that the person reclining on the couch was his brother, nor did it indicate the

---

[6] *Swan on a Black Sea*, pages 33-34.

relationship of the apparition to him. However, at about the time when Geraldine was writing this script Mr and Mrs Salter were reading an account of the incident (presumably from the above Proceedings), so telepathy between the living may account for a part, though not all of the account which Geraldine penned. Arthur Balfour had indeed been deeply in love with Catherine Mary Lyttelton, and was on the point of declaring himself, when the latter contracted typhus fever and died on Palm Sunday March 21st 1875 at the age of 25. The event shattered him. He remained unmarried all his life, was accustomed to visit Fisher Hill whenever the anniversary of her death came round to remember her in silence, and had an ornamental box made to contain a tress of her hair, cut off after her death. This, like the true identity of 'Mrs Willett', was kept a closely guarded family secret throughout the whole of Arthur Balfour's life, not revealed till thirty years after his death when it was printed as *The Palm Sunday Case* in the above-mentioned volume of the SPR Proceedings, which detailed a number of other occasions when it appeared to be mentioned, though obscurely, in various automatic scripts.

This romantic story was, according to Geraldine, not known to her; she had not read Gerald Balfour's Study. If one is not willing to impugn her veracity (as I do not), super-ESP seems the only way of explaining the accurate details of an as yet unpublished event, if discarnate contact is ruled out.

A second extract, from the tenth script, has evidential touches but is interesting more for its manifestation of human feeling. The communicator is describing her courtship.

> 'What's in a name?' says Shakespeare. Everything when one falls in love. Mine was not a sudden, swift fall. It was a slow- motion picture in this film of memory. When Charles came to figure in my life, how shy I was of him! He seemed much too old for me. I had experience of undergraduates who were far too young. I was very flattered by his attentions but did not believe that they were more than kindness to the rather 'out-of-it' girl.
>
> Strangely they persisted, but they were oblique. In other words he was cautious and, as I later realised, he was apprehensive of the criticisms of his women-folk. Poor Charles, he was family-ridden then; I think I'm glad, H., that you are free in that sense.

What is called a united family is an un-natural phenomenon. An Englishman who quarrels with his family is following a natural healthy instinct. It does not matter who or what started the quarrel, they are obeying nature's law in casting each other off.

I was very nervous, too, and therefore rather elusive during that courtship. But it became amusing to me and gave me self-confidence. When Charles began to arrange for us to meet by subterfuge, while he would ignore me almost to rudeness while we were in the company of others, at first I took it all lightly.

Then he became serious, ardent. He could not conceal from me his deep feelings any longer and suddenly love woke up. He swept the young girl off her feet. The old, old woman can only write of it now because she has been watching it scene by scene, living again its varied emotions, its keen anxieties, its palpitating wonder, its fears, its hopes, and yet remaining detached, the spectator in the stalls. Oh my dear, you do not know your mother, or rather you only know one aspect of her, the role she played as mother in your life, and a very busy mother too.

The family didn't like the choice of their Charles. Eveleen and Dorothy were distinctly disdainful, patronising. They were fashionable married women. I was the young nobody. My prospective M. in L. alarmed me absurdly at first. I, the sophisticated old Dame, surveyed this comedy of memory re-enacted, saw how his women-folk's attitude spurred on Charles, when they tried so hard to put him off. I was dazzled, enchanted, uplifted by his increasing devotion. And though very hurt, I was determined to show the family I was not a nobody by any means.[7]

    There, in brief outline, is a story which, filled out by a competent romantic novelist, has the ingredients of a bestseller - though perhaps it might be necessary to lower the age of the hero below his unromantic forty-two.
    The whole series of scripts, after having been edited by Signe Toksvig, a friend of Geraldine's and herself an authority on another distinguished psychic, Emmanuel Swedenborg, and with added comments

---

[7] *Swan on a Black Sea*, pages 44-45.

on significant passages or statements by persons whom the scripts concerned or who had special knowledge about the events referred to in them, was prefaced by a foreword from Professor Charles Broad, a Fellow of Trinity College, Cambridge and a noted psychical researcher. It is clear from his comments that he was considerably impressed. He had been associated with many of the persons named in the scripts during his career in the University and had been a tutor of Mrs Coombe Tennant's youngest son; he had also met that lady a few times, but had no suspicion at all that she was also 'Mrs Willett'. His Foreword presents the biographical background of Mrs Coombe Tennant's career in considerable detail, first as she was known to her family, friends and acquaintances, and then in regard to her secret activities as 'Mrs Willett'. Having set these out, he gave his own impressions and reactions. He first considered how close to fact the verifiable statements in the scripts were.

> Statements made by the ostensible communicator about her experiences at the point of death or in the afterlife cannot be tested. Nor can some of the statements about the emotions she felt towards certain persons and in certain situations in her earthly life. But, when all these are set aside, there remains a large mass of statements which can be tested. And, in marked contrast to the contents of many mediumistic utterances, they are not in the least vague, general, allusive or oracular. They abound in extremely concrete detail about named persons and places, and about definite events in which these were concerned.
>
> Moreover, of the large mass of concrete testable statements, very nearly all are true. And when a mistake in detail is made ... it is nearly always corrected in a later script.[8]

He then went on to consider the dramatic form in which the scripts were presented.

> No reader could fail to get the impression of an extremely definite personality, with a rather unusual combination of characteristics. In one aspect she is a typical Victorian *grande dame*, who treats even her 'unseen guests' as she was wont to treat ordinary mortals in her capacity of hostess; who likes to play her part in public life, and does

---

[8] *Swan on a Black Sea*, Foreword, page xliv.

so very efficiently; and whose political interests are surprisingly radical for a woman of her period and social position. In another aspect she has very strong likes and dislikes towards certain individuals; and, in particular, she has an intense maternal instinct, and an uneasy feeling that this has not always been fortunate in its effects on her relationships with her children. In yet another aspect, she is a mystic, possessed of psychic gifts which she has for long been concerned to conceal ... It is for those who knew Mrs Coombe Tennant intimately, and, in particular, for her surviving sons, to decide whether the very marked personality which emerges in the scripts is that of the individual who is ostensibly communicating through Geraldine Cummins. All that I can usefully say is that it seems to me, as a largely but not wholly ignorant external observer, to fit like a glove.[9]

He next enquires what might be the least unplausible way of explaining the production of the scripts if one considers only normal sources of information and generally recognised abilities of cognition, selection and dramatisation in the writer, and ended

> I do not see how we can explain, without postulating something paranormal, the amount and kind of detailed and correct information, highly relevant to Mrs Coombe Tennant, that had already emerged by the end of the sixth script.[10]

He goes on to consider how far telepathy from living persons might sufficiently explain the contents of the scripts.

So far as the facts adduced were concerned, this might be so, though he points out that there is no independent evidence for telepathy on such a grand scale, or for clairvoyance which could read so many existing printed records. When it came to explaining how such telepathically and clairvoyantly acquired information could then be presented in a dramatic form so characteristic of the deceased person, this too could not be parallelled from previous experience.

> Obviously much the simplest and most plausible hypothesis *prima facie*, is that Mrs Coombe Tennant, or some aspect of her, survived the death of her body on August 31st 1956; that she was still actively

---

[9] *Swan on a Black Sea*, Foreword, pages xliv-xlv.
[10] *Ibid.*, p. xlvi.

in existence at least as late as March 1960, and that during that period she from time to time controlled, directly or indirectly, the pen of the automatist. On the other hand, it seems to most contemporary Westerners[11] antecedently improbable, to the point of practical inconceivability, that a person should continue to exist and to function after the death and disintegration of his earthly body, with its brain and nervous system. It is only because of this that so many of the few who are aware of the kind of facts of which the present case is such a striking instance, and who are prepared honestly to face them, have recourse to the fantastic hypothesis, involving telepathy and clairvoyance on the part of those still in the flesh, which I have described in discussing the second alternative type of explanation.[12]

Sitting thus uneasily on the fence, he allows that some sort of conscious survival is the most plausible hypothesis, and on this assumption makes some observations of his own, particularly noting that the society reflected in the scripts appeared to present only a narrow and peculiar corner of the after-world - one peopled by cultured and intelligent members of the English upper classes over a certain brief span of history - and that little that is bad or unpleasant appears in what looks like a rose-tinted account.

It is not possible within the confines of this chapter to do anything like justice to this remarkable sequence of communications. The book in which they appear is essential reading for anyone who wishes to estimate the likelihood that some human beings survive bodily death. One's final conclusions will largely depend on the mental attitude one brings to the reading. No evidence so far forthcoming from mediumistic sources has ever provided the sort of one hundred percent conviction that can follow from, let us say, the proof of a proposition in Euclid. However, assurance can come from evidence that is less than one hundred per cent. When making important decisions in ordinary life we are content with evidence that is highly probable - the sort which could bring about a conviction in a court of law. With regard to the Coombe Tennant scripts one thinks of an identity-establishing

---

[11] Most contemporary Westerners? One might take issue with Professor Broad here. Most Westerners are probably religionists of one sort of another, Christians of Orthodox, Catholic, Anglican or Protestant persuasion, together with a large number of Jews and (since Professor Broad's time) Moslems, for all of whom some doctrine of survival of death is fundamental to their faith.

[12] *Swan on a Black Sea*, pages xlix-l.

suit such as the Tichborne Case. Something like this was what Mrs Coombe Tennant appeared to be doing for the benefit of her sceptical son Henry. Had she been bringing it in a terrestrial court of law she would surely have won her case.

Dr Robert Thouless, reviewing the book in the SPR *Journal*, thought it strengthened the case for belief in survival.

> It would, I think, be a mistake to judge this book as if its importance lay in providing conclusive proof of the survival of Mrs Coombe Tennant; no set of scripts could do that. Evidence from information can always in principle be explained by the unconscious memory of the medium or by her paranormal capacities for ESP and pre-cognition. Evidence from recognition can also never be coercive since we can never be sure that we know the limits of the medium's capacity for unconscious dramatic construction. The best that we can expect from a set of scripts is that such explanations may become very unlikely ones.
>
> If then we ask a different question and enquire whether this book adds to the weight of evidence for post-mortem communication from a surviving personality, I think that the answer should be that it certainly does. The scripts can be most easily explained if we suppose that Mrs Tennant has survived and that she played at least a part in their production.[13]

For what it is worth, the present writer's feeling is that he would go a little further than Broad or Thouless and plump decisively for the authenticity of these scripts as emanating from the surviving mind of Mrs Coombe Tennant. True, we can never know the extent to which telepathy from the living and clairvoyance of existing written material may have contributed to their production, or what Geraldine may have heard or overheard or noticed in reading and then forgotten. Equally, we cannot know how much her dramatic faculty may have fleshed out the bare factual bones derived from such sources into a personality which was found recognisable by those who knew her. We cannot know, only estimate a likelihood. The likelihood seems strong enough to me to warrant belief.

---

[13] *Journal of the SPR*, Volume for March 1966, page 270.

13

REFLECTIONS AND CONCLUSIONS

Geraldine Cummins, once a psychic phenomenon, is now a part of psychic history. Her career spanned the period between the age of the founders of psychical research, who had high hopes of discovering scientifically reputable proofs, and perhaps explanations of anomalous happenings - especially human survival of bodily death - and the present age of more subdued and somewhat disheartened interest.

Among the automatists studied by the SPR she stands out as perhaps the most important, with a huge output of paranormally produced script to her credit, some of which certainly contains evidence of extra-sensory perception and, many would believe, of genuine discarnate communication.

Whether or not the latter was really the case is the question that most urgently asks itself because of its human implications. Alternative explanations for apparent messages from the dead can always be found if one is prepared to fetch them from far enough, without impugning her honesty. As time passes there will no doubt be some who are ready to do that as well once all those who knew her have mouldered away; fraud, however humanly unlikely that seems now to those who knew her, along with cryptomnesia (which can almost never be disproved) and the fantastic suppositions of super-ESP will be held to explain all.

The present writer was attracted to the idea of writing an appreciation of Geraldine Cummins because he himself happens to be a practising automatist. He is also a practising minister of religion (though at the age of seventy-five not very heavily committed). Whether Geraldine herself would have wished one of the latter to write about her, since she sat lightly to the established religion of the Church of Ireland in which she had been brought up, is perhaps questionable, but she would probably not have objected to one of the former, though my own abilities in automatic writing are not to be compared with hers. They have, however, helped me to understand her. My *curriculum vitae* before and during my priesthood in the Anglican Communion, and my own discovery of a psychic ability at the age of fifty-seven have been described elsewhere and need not here be enlarged upon.

Most practising Christians of all denominations, except for a few mavericks (I forbear from mentioning names) accept as axiomatic that personal conscious life continues after bodily death; the individual remains to give an account of himself before his Maker (whatever that metaphor may correspond with in future fact). This is implied in the Nicene Creed: *I look for the resurrection of the dead and the life of the world to come.* Difficulties may be felt about that, as about other elements of the Creed as verbally expressed, and the ways in which resurrection is envisaged differ widely, but faith in a Risen Christ makes no sense at all if Christ has not risen, if the whole personality of Jesus vanished utterly when he died. One cannot be a Christian in the sense that one can be a Platonist or a Marxist, holding views similar to theirs, whether or not they still exist. Being a Christian means belonging to a community which has a living head; belonging to it one is infused by his living Spirit.

Experience of membership of the living Body of Christ conveys with it the assurance of spiritual life, whatever views the separate members may hold about the imperfections and fallibility of that body's human representatives or the questionable reliability of the written records which have[1] been preserved as the foundation documents of the faith. It is possible for a very sceptical person to be a Christian - or so it seems to me, for I am one. One might compare the Christian faith to a three-legged stool, the three legs being continuance in corporate worship (the activity of the Body through which spiritual life is mediated), persistence in personal prayer (which implies belief in a God who hears; one cannot pray to a nothing) and the practice of the agreed Christian life-style (which includes charity and humility as well

---

[1] See *A Hand in Dialogue*, C. E. J. Fryer. James Clarke & Co., Cambridge, 1983.

REFLECTIONS AND CONCLUSIONS

as being somewhat tough with oneself: Christianity is not a prigs' charter). Such a stool will support its sitter on any sort of ground, however uneven; if you insist in attaching a fourth leg the stool will not remain firm but wobble.

No doubt the sort of resurrection envisaged by the earliest Christians, of a Master disappearing upwards into the sky, whither they would eventually follow Him and whence they would eventually return with Him, was a product of their own thinking and world-view, natural to them, impossible for us. The accounts of the re-appearances of Jesus after he had been crucified and buried, which assured his disciples that he was not dead but alive, have been mulled over again and again, some seeing the events as entirely physical, others as a matter of spiritual conviction expressed in physical terms. Some have thought there were no such events but that the stories we have are imaginative pictures invented by the early Church to express their inward experience. But it is perhaps not without significance that all the unusual features of the 'forty days' can be paralleled in what recorders of psychical events have noted down in reports made at one time or another to the SPR - even the disappearance and re-appearance of parts of a human body.

If anyone wishes to explain the resurrection appearances of Jesus in this way, as events in the psychic rather than the physical order, I cannot see any objection to it. The question at issue is not how they happened but whether they happened. Being a Christian involves being convinced that the foundation-event of the faith, the death of Jesus and its subsequent reversal, was a real event; how it happened is irrelevant to faith.

Jesus' resurrection implies and (for the Christian) guarantees the resurrection of the dead in general - a point insisted on very strongly by the first Biblical writer to mention it.

However 'Resurrection' is understood, it implies that one survives death. For this reason the study of mediumistic utterances ought not to be ruled out as undeserving of consideration by Christian thinkers - though they need to have their wits about them while they consider. Reports of continued conscious life after death, supported by what seems good evidence (even if it merely consists of anecdotes which happen to be strikingly apt) ought to interest them, and frequently they do. Many, however, shrink from having anything to do with such things, believing that they cannot but be manifestations of evil spiritual influences, and regarding those through whom the evidence comes as tools of the devil, used to mislead people with specious lies. Since it cannot be supposed that someone lending himself or herself to possession by a demonic agency would fail to show signs in his or her personality of evil influence, and since after fifty-five years of such association Geraldine showed no such signs, but remained a basically good person, and since no medium I have known has shown such progressive deterioration of character, I shall ignore this as a likelihood, and briefly consider what relevance her disclosures may have for those who adhere to basic Christian convictions.

First, however, to change hats for a moment, removing the ecclesiastical biretta and assuming that of the psychic. (A witch's hat? I hope not.) My reactions during the two years during which this book has been in preparation, both to Geraldine's personality and to her automatically-written scripts as compared and contrasted with my own, have been chiefly those of enormous respect for an ability far superior to mine. Devoting her energies increasingly to its practice, she produced material not only in great quantity but of high quality, which culminated in the series described in the last chapter. I have myself no such development to show after eighteen years of practice. To some extent our methods and experience have been different. Unlike Geraldine, I am never conscious of an alteration in my mental state when I write. Also I have, probably, a more cluttered mind, concerned with the interests of a student of history, a writer of books on railways and a practising minister in the Episcopal Church of Scotland. She, I fancy, had fewer such distractions and therefore less mental undergrowth through which ideas originated from outside had to penetrate. It is plausible to me that my chief communicator is (so he claims) the spirit of my father; how plausible it was to her that 'Astor' and 'Silenio', her two chief controls, were genuinely once-incarnate human personalities I do not know. Beatrice Gibbes had no doubts about it but her friend seems not to have been so sure. It is conceivable that with each of us the controlling agency is an aspect of the writer's mind behaving as if it were a separate intelligence. Admitting it to work within oneself does not seem to have done either of us any damage.

However, the significant thing about whoever or whatever controlled Geraldine's hand when she wrote was his, or its ability to make accurate statements about matters of which she had no knowledge through the normal use of her senses.

The Ambrose Pratt case may serve as an example. Geraldine had not, so far as she knew, heard of him. Yet with a little assistance from allusive imagery his name came out in the course of a minute or so. This is something I cannot match, so far as I can remember, in my own experience.

Could it have been a consequence of fraud? It is of course conceivable that she pretended to write it automatically after spending some time researching. Perhaps she asked questions over the long-distance telephone to someone she knew in Australia and eventually obtained information which she carefully composed into a bogus message. But such an explanation lacks plausibility. She was not a rich woman; where would she find the money for such an extensive 'phone call? It is not as if she were being paid for her services. Did she keep a fund for the purpose? Why should she beggar herself on an exercise which brought nothing in return but the kind of kick which one might privately gain from deceiving somebody? Was she that sort of person? In any case, no such easy explanation fits the Marguerite Le Hand case; there, we should have to suppose a conspiracy between David Gray and herself, at enormous risk to his career if it were discovered, and with no conceivable gain for either party.

Can telepathy between the living be called in to explain such cases? We know it happens, and that it appears to be independent of distance and sometimes precognitive. Did Geraldine explore Raynor Johnson's mind as they conversed over afternoon tea on the occasion when he came to visit her in London? Did she focus on David Gray in her spare time, and rummage around in his mind and memory for something interesting to intrigue her friend Beatrice Gibbes? But if one allows telepathy, especially this sort of free-lance telepathy, one has to postulate something which is as unbelievable to the protesting sceptic as the survival of an active mind after the brain has disintegrated. If Geraldine could cognise Raynor Johnson or David Gray at a distance, then her mind was operating apart from her physical brain; leaving Chelsea, it travels to Melbourne or Dublin. But if it cannot exist apart from the brain, how can it leave the brain? And if it so obviously does operate apart from the brain, what is there to prevent it from existing and operating when the brain dies? The established facts of telepathy make the axioms of the sceptic implausible.

There is surely nothing illogical or preposterous in the belief held by highly intelligent thinkers in all ages, that, in Plato's phrase, 'the soul is immortal'. Such an hypothesis fits the facts not only of psychic encounters but also of those near-death experiences of which Plato's 'Myth of Er' at the end of his Republic is perhaps an imaginatively-embroidered example. Of course the survival hypothesis can never be proved beyond any shadow of doubt. But it does, to my mind, seem a far more probable alternative, and I think I should opt for it quite apart from such religious propensities as I possess. In this life one bases one's convictions on probabilities; one has to or one could scarcely live. Human society would be impossible if one demanded absolute incontrovertible proof of everyone else's trustworthiness before committing oneself to them. I would not find fault with an agnostic who felt he could not believe in an afterlife when the proofs were not completely compelling, but it would be fair to point out to him that in day-to-day living he does not demand such proofs.

I am trying to make the point that it is reasonable to believe in survival of death. One transfers the habits of belief during earthly life to a wider sphere - that is all.

Evidence that would make me feel sure that someone I knew is now resident in a country I have never myself been to would be good evidence still, even if that were the 'undiscovered country from whose bourne no traveller returns'. Possibly I am wrong. Possibly death is as final as it seemed to be to the Preacher in the Book of Ecclesiastes: *The living know that they will die, but the dead know nothing.*

There are no more rewards for them; they are utterly forgotten.[2] Possibly, on the mental and spiritual level, everything ends in nothing.

Possibly, but not, I think, probably. It seems to me that non-survivalism is very much a matter of mood. The pampered rich man, like the Preacher in the Old Testament (whoever he may have been) sated with the good things of this life until they fail to please him any more, having lapsed into a mixture of depression and resignation, extends it forward into the grave. Nothing is really worth having here, so let us not hanker after anything there. Whereas the victims of poverty or injustice, like the slaves on the American cotton plantations, are less likely to feel that way; a just God, they feel, will give them redress in another life; oh, to be over Jordan! Both viewpoints may be wish orientated - which is not to say that neither can be true. But parapsychological findings do give hints and inklings, at the least, that the more hopeful view is the true one.

As to the value of such findings, that, I suppose, is a matter of personal judgement, for they cannot be measured or weighed. To take two of Geraldine's script-sequences - the chief two, as it seems to me - those purportedly from Myers and Mrs Coombe Tennant. They are very, very

---

[2] Ecclesiastes 9, v. 5.

different. No one coming to them for the first time, who did not know how they originated, would have attributed them to the same person. The first is expository and philosophical, ranging as widely as can be imagined - as widely as Plato ever ranged. The second is vigorous and sometimes passionate utterance, full of one-sided attitudes not yet discarded and human feelings still cherished, the garrulous conversation of an upper-class Englishwoman ranging over the whole course of a remembered human life. Both came from the pen of a moderately-educated Irishwoman writing in light trance without pauses for reflection. Remembering the other personalities (or quasi-personalities) who also wrote through her - the puzzled 'Mallory', the restless 'Lawrence', the savant 'Ambrose Pratt', not to mention the 'Messenger' of the Cleophas scripts with his 'ye olde' diction and the strangely-compelling 'Fawcett' in whom Geraldine could not bring herself to believe - if these were not visitants but components of her mind, what an extraordinary person this rather unassuming woman must have been.

To return to discussing the relevance of Geraldine's disclosures to Christian belief and faith. What emerges from them, and from the 'Myers' scripts in particular, is a pattern of stages of discarnate life, each of indefinite duration, in the earliest of which continued conscious individual life bears much resemblance to earthly life, purged of unpleasantness, and is for each experiment very much what he or she chooses to make it. This it seems is the case with the general run of ordinary people; evidence is scanty for what happens to those whose characters were unsatisfactory or downright evil when on earth, though occasionally such individuals put in an appearance, still manifesting the bad qualities which they showed during life - jealousy, malevolence and so on; she dismissed such characters as soon as she could. As the surviving soul continues to dwell in a world of pleasurable illusion, after a while it either chooses to return to earth or senses that there are fuller existences beyond its present level; in the latter case a desire to progress causes it to choose to set out on an upward path (to use a spatial metaphor), the stages along which are characterised by the increasing cooperating of like-minded persons, leading eventually to a fusion of personalities in a larger personality.

The ultimate goal is union with the Divine Spirit, though this seems to be an ultimate possibility rather than a likelihood - and in any event such a consummation is impossible to describe.

Does this conflict with the doctrines of the Christian Church? It is difficult to say, except in regard to the return of souls to the earth, which orthodox Christianity has usually firmly rejected as a part of the Divine plan. Apart from this, one cannot easily fit the Church pattern against the psychical pattern (as set out by 'Myers' and others) as one would check a product against its template. While asserting the reality of a life after death, both for the just and the unjust, the New Testament writers have been reticent as to details, and much of what they did say was cast into symbolic form.

A good deal of popular misunderstanding has arisen from regarding passages from the Book of Revelation as descriptive of an afterlife - for example that the blessed dead will play harps, wear robes which have been 'washed white in the blood of the Lamb', (a contradiction in terms if taken literally) and inhabit a city whose gates are made of pearl and whose streets are paved with gold. The Revelation is a visionary and apocalyptic book and no more to be taken literally than Dante's *Paradiso*. Jesus himself said very little (or at any rate is recorded as having said very little) about the post-resurrection life. He clearly believed there was one, ranging himself in this respect on the side of the Pharisees, who affirmed it, rather than of the Sadducees, who denied it, and he indicated that relationships between 'those who are accounted worthy to attain to the resurrection' would be different then from what they are now, but his teaching was mainly about The Kingdom of God', a term not easy to translate but seemingly referring to a state of human society where God's lordship would be universally recognised, 'on earth as in heaven'.

A good deal of misunderstanding also arises from taking statements in hymns literally (and more people probably sing or have sung hymns with some frequency than have listened intently to sermons or have read their Bibles closely). Hymns are poetry (sometimes bad poetry) and largely express themselves in symbols, or exercise poetic licence so greatly as to be completely at variance with Scriptural statements. (E.g: 'Gentle Jesus, meek and mild . . .' - referring to the man who angrily drove out the moneychangers from the Temple with a whip of cords!) The realities of the afterlife - or, as the New Testament terms it, 'the Resurrection of the dead!' - are according to those who have tried to speak across the divide impossible to explain in terms familiar to ourselves, and have to be mediated through simile and metaphor. Something similar is found in the New Testament scriptures. On no occasion is a Christian who has died described as speaking from beyond death, though Jesus is more than once recorded as speaking directly to one of his servants - as in the case of St Paul's conversion on the Damascus road. The writer of the Letter to the Hebrews speaks of past heroic characters of Hebrew history looking on, like spectators at athletic games, watching the performances of their successors. (But perhaps this is not more than a literary device.) Christians who have died are spoken of as 'sleeping', which suggests survival with consciousness in abeyance, but here, too, it may be simply metaphor. There is a general reticence as to details.

However, such a scheme as 'Myers' outlines in his two script-sequences is not inconsistent with Christian insights. St Paul, in particular, speaks of going 'from glory to glory' which suggests progression, and in one place he speaks of someone (probably though not certainly himself) who had been 'caught up into paradise and heard words so secret that human lips may not repeat them',[3] and this may perhaps be understood as meaning they were incommunicable.

One has to remember, in reading the New Testament, that its earlier writers believed that Jesus would be returning very soon to bring in the kingdom of God on earth, and that this filled their imaginations, not the prospect of surviving death. St Paul's Epistles reflect this belief - the ones that may be safely considered, from stylistic evidence, as genuinely his productions.[4] This expectation lessened as the years went by, but direct evidence of the 'resurrection life' was not apparently sought. The background atmosphere was different from that of our own day. No one, or almost no one, questioned that people survived death, though only a minority supposed that the survival was that of a whole personality. There were innumerable gods and demons galore. Nowadays - in Western civilisation, at any rate, it is not a choice between different sorts of gods and one God, but between the latter and no God, no afterlife, no ultimate meaning.

As to human reincarnation - and the allied notion that one may have pre-existed one's life on this earth in some spiritual region, and definitely chosen to be born as a human being: the Church as a whole, through declarations of its councils, rejected these ideas. One of the early Church Fathers, the third-century Origen, was severely criticised for supporting pre-existence. Only Jesus Christ was believed to have pre-existed his human life. However, these two ideas are not so much

---

[3] See II. Corinthians 12, v. 4. It reads like a reference to a 'near death experience' which may well have happened when Paul was stoned and left for dead during one of his missionary journeys - see Acts 14, vv. 19-20.

[4] These include the Epistles to the Romans, the Corinthians (2), the Galatians and the Thessalonians (2) along with the short Epistle to Philemon.

denied in the Christian scriptures as overlooked. For myself, I regard them as possibilities. I do not see why we should be so sure that they cannot be part of God's will for men and women. 'Myers' distinguishes between eastern reincarnational beliefs, of reincarnation occurring again and again and being a sort of wheel of continued misery, and his own belief that it happened to individuals occasionally. In regard to reincarnation, there can of course be no proof, for any supposed evidence can be otherwise explained.[5] So I do not think it can be confidently asserted or denied; in this matter I sit firmly on the fence.

Reincarnation would certainly help to explain and make more bearable many of the apparent injustices of life - but that does not mean that it is true.

In general, and apart from the 'Myers' scripts, purportedly delivered from 'Eidos', and the 'Cleophas' communications, the messages given to Geraldine seem to have emanated from the lower reaches of the life to come, in which recognisable people, still very much their old selves, continue in a kind of idealised human life and in general find it very acceptable. Very much that she was given was for the relief of grief, and this of course meant contacting the recently departed. Her unconsciously-conducted researches were limited in scope. If there are, as Jesus is reported to have said, many resting-places in his Father's house, she was mostly in touch with only the nearest, applying her ear, so to speak, to the keyhole of the front door into the entrance hall. From this nearer region came the most convincing disclosures, glimpses, if 'Myers' is to be credited, of an illusory territory beyond which the authentic realms of discarnate life extend, to be discovered later. She does not provide material for a thoroughgoing survey of the life to come, except insofar as the 'Myers' scripts adumbrate one.

As to the plausibility of the latter, each reader must make up his own mind; they certainly impress me. If her disclosures, though narrow in scope, are genuine, however, they do seem to be important. There is a bridge across the chasm whose further side we cannot see. People cross the Jordan, they are not engulfed in its waters. And they remain themselves after they have crossed.

The discarnate contacts she made were introduced by 'Astor' and 'Silenio' - in most cases by the former. Who or what were they? Miss

---

[5] For example, a young child may claimed to recognise persons he has never met, and refer accurately to things about them, but telepathic precognition mistaken for reincarnational memory could explain this.

Gibbes, in a privately printed booklet produced at some time in the later 'thirties (it bears no date) gives her reasons for believing that they were once-human beings, distinct from each other and from Geraldine. They were certainly an odd pair. 'Astor' claimed to be an ancient Greek, formerly a disciple of Plotinus; he had a contempt both for Christians and Jews, whom he apparently lumped together, and expresses his dislike frequently. 'Silenio' said he had been a slave who had become a Christian and had suffered for his faith in the arena at Rome. He had not been born until after the deaths of the earliest Christian apostles.

This would place his career perhaps late in the first or early in the second century; 'Astor's' would have been late in the third or early in the fourth century. (Miss Gibbes talks about them having been 'on earth round about 2,000 years ago', a curious lapse in an otherwise careful woman.) The two did not appear to get on well. Occasionally they argued for the control of the medium's hand. The difference between the proud and arrogant 'Astor' and the meek and mild 'Silenio' persuaded Beatrice Gibbes that they must be different entities. She did not find the suggestion that they were subliminal creations owing their separate identities to Geraldine a plausible explanation, because 'Miss Cummins is no actress'. But this is beside the point. Deep down she may well have been, as our dreams tell us we all are, a very good dramatiser indeed. It is to me plausible that the pro and anti-Christian who appeared and conducted slanging matches (most of the slang coming from the supercilious 'Astor') when she was engaged in writing the Cleophas scripts were in fact aspects of herself, and that the polemic expressed viewpoints that she had repressed. She had been brought up in the Church of Ireland and conducted to church every Sunday, to listen to long sermons and Biblical readings. There is no indication in anything she herself wrote afterwards, or in anything that was told me, that she had any wish to continue to do this once she became an independent adult. But when at home at Woodville she regularly accompanied her mother to church, merely to please her. The obedient child and the determinedly- independent adult were perhaps always at odds. 'Astor' represented her adult self which had broken free, 'Silenio' the child who had, for a while, been broken in, but who sank out of sight and then re-appeared while she was writing on a quasi-scriptural theme.

I think it is arguable that these two controls reflected inwardly-conflicting parts of her deeper mind. One notes that 'Silenio' disappeared once the Cleophas scripts had all been written, and left 'Astor' in possession of the field. One notes, too, that it was through 'Astor' that she was given evidential material. It would be interesting if an investigation of her mediumship could be made by someone as intelligent and perceptive as Eleanor Sidgwick (who wrote about Mrs Piper) or Gerald Balfour (who did the same for 'Mrs Willett'). The written material is still there, in the archives at Cork. It is also interesting to note that in Script 36 of the Coombe Tennant sequence, dated July 16th 1959, the communicator refers to 'G.C.'s subliminal mind, which is called "Astor".' This suggests by implication that Geraldine herself had doubts - as all honest automatists sometimes have.

It is time to sum up. What, over fifty years of psychic involvement, did Geraldine Cummins achieve, and was it worth the sacrifice of her creative talent? Any aspiring writer, faced with the option of creating from his own personal resources or of being the passive instrument of unknown ghostly entities, would surely choose the former if the choice were completely free. The urge to write books, of whatever kind, and receive recognition and approval from one's fellows, is a very powerful stimulus - comparable, perhaps, to the wish to have a child of one's own. Geraldine certainly had such a desire from an early age. Then, when she was about twenty-five, came the realisation that she had psychic gifts as well. Could the two abilities co-exist? She seems for a while to have thought so.

But the appearance of Beatrice Gibbes on the scene tilted the balance in favour of the psychic. The latter, it well may have been, ate into the energies needed for the former and her independent productiveness lessened. Eventually, realising that her paranormal productions were so astonishing, both in quantity and quality, she suffered the former to predominate, and eventually bowed to pressure from her friend to concentrate exclusively on them. Beatrice Gibbes died soon afterwards, but the promise had been given and she felt impelled to keep it. The natural creative talent withered, the psychic one flourished, to culminate in the remarkable Coombe Tennant scripts.

Was it worth it? Did she do more for her contemporaries than if she had become a novelist or playwright? She seems to have felt that the ability to bring comfort to bereaved people was something that mattered greatly, more than a propensity for writing stories about Irish life and character.

One cannot weigh imponderables against each other, but if one believes that one reason for being in this life at all is that one should do good to others, the latter is surely not as important as the former. Only a few writers of fiction give more to their readers than pleasure and amusement and the where-withal to pass an idle hour. These greater spirits, without preaching or being didactic, do something more, passing on values as desirable, life-styles as worth assuming; they can modify the personality as well as pleasing it. The Jane Austens and George Eliots of the writing world can do this. That was why the Greeks valued Homer and the Romans Virgil. Moral amelioration is added to mental pleasure; one is the better for reading them. But Geraldine, who had no great opinion of herself, probably knew she would never be in that category.

However, it was her lot to live in an age when something precious was being increasingly extinguished - religious hope. For centuries this had been (along with, it has to be admitted, religious terror) an element in the minds of the common man and woman. Innumerable old gravestones express the expectation of immortality. But with the rise of scientific knowledge (inevitable and good so far as it went) and the spread of materialistic philosophies which supposedly fitted it, religious belief declined; clouds came across the sun. Sensitive souls felt the deprivation; Tennyson and Matthew Arnold expressed their sense of loss memorably in their verse. Less sensitive persons gloried in the change. 'Pie in the sky when you die' was as childish an expectation as it was unlikely. Human progress was inevitable. Life on earth would become more and more enjoyable.

Religion would disappear when its consolations were no longer felt necessary. You could have the pie now instead of having to wait for it. Then came the First World War, and the dreams of inevitable progress disappeared; at the same time religious convictions were even further undermined.

Men who could behave like wild beasts towards one another were obviously not progressing - and belief in a God who could allow such things to happen also took a knock. Church congregations dwindled. The laws of Moses no longer seemed to be binding. Pie in the sky seemed more and more unlikely, and only a few could enjoy pie now. Resentments among the defeated built up towards a Second World War.

The clouds returned after the rain. Ordinary human hopefulness disappeared; war was followed by cold war. The hope of immortality was already something many people had discarded.

It may seem strange that an accredited minister of religion should approve the re-kindling of hope through psychic discovery. It is certainly true that most churches regarded the psychic dimension as something nasty in the woodshed, a deceptive by-meadow into which only the foolish would stray. An Anglican archbishop during the 'thirties deliberately suppressed a Report compiled by a Committee of his own Church because it was too favourable to Spiritualism.

However, if psychic events happen at all, it seems to me that a religiously-inclined person should regard them as a part of God's universal ordering, and if their tendency is on the whole good, if they favour human virtue, if they appear to produce, however anomalously, the fruits of the Spirit, then they should be welcomed and, if possible, baptised into Christian usage. This was what happened in the Early Church when the phenomenon of 'speaking with tongues' arose. If someone appears to be gifted with the sort of insight which suggests that the Christian hope of immortality is real, that the dead do not die and that many live on in a *milieu* of joy and fulfilment, then surely the right thing to do is to examine and test that person in a positive manner, seeking to establish above all that good and not harm come from his or her activities. That is, to follow the advice of Jesus and judge the tree by its fruits.

Now there have been people who, having psychic abilities, have misused them for evil purposes. I do not think Geraldine can be classed among these. People came to her for hope and comfort who would not have listened to any cleric; that was the Church's fault for losing credibility. She gave the conviction that their dead were really alive. One can of course maintain that the evidence she offered did not come from their departed loved ones at all, but had been gained in some roundabout manner through telepathy or clairvoyance. If that were the case, then we have a very peculiar ethical situation. Lies and delusions can make people happier, remove grief, enable human life to be lived without being overshadowed by despair. Humbug gives hope! There seems to me to be a built-in contradiction here.

'The truth shall make you free', Jesus said. May one reverse this and say that what sets someone free must in some measure be true? Here is something for philosophers and specialists in ethics to argue about. The fact remains that to dozens of enquirers Geraldine gave hope, which they could not have gained from another source.

One can of course say to a grieving person, 'You must accept that the person you loved is now completely gone. You must endeavour to cope with your grief and perhaps find that other loves and affections will soften the bitterness of the memory. This is part of the human condition which cannot be escaped.' That is how a humanist would reply, and some strong-minded persons could no doubt take it. Or one could say, 'The Church assures you that there is hope. You will meet your loved one again through the mercy of God. That assurance should be enough for you. Here are some passages in the Bible; go home and study them.' In former times that would have satisfied most people. That is not the case now. But if someone can be found who can say, 'Your loved one survives, and here are some special reasons for believing it, facts which I was told and which you will recognise,' the effect can be like that upon St Thomas, when the marks of the wounds proved to him that he really was in his Master's presence. This kind of assurance can convince even simple and un-religious people, who know nothing of either philosophy because their own experience has never encompassed such studies.

I once introduced to a spiritualist medium, whose gifts and personal character I respected, to a middle-aged woman whose nineteen-year-old daughter had died in a tragic accident.

She was grieving very badly. The medium told her certain things which left her convinced that Elizabeth was still alive. She said to me afterwards, I should have gone to the grave a bitter old woman, but Mrs E. has given me hope.' I have also to confess that, although I came into the Church in my forties after study and reflection, and later took orders within it, full conviction of the reality of 'the life of the world to come' only reached me through psychic sources.

What does good is good. That is the justification for Geraldine's persistence in the practice of the psychic gift.

She helped many to recover hope, and harmed no one. Of how many statesmen or stateswomen could that be said, who go to their graves loaded with honours? Nobody, so far as I know, has ever been decorated for the exercise of a psychic gift. Geraldine might well have hooted with laughter at the notion. Perhaps it is as well that she should have been a prophet without honour, leaving behind instead the name of someone whose actions smell sweet and blossom in the dust.

APPENDIX
THE NON-PSYCHIC WRITINGS

Apart from automatically-written material published at various times in a number of volumes and two early plays written in collaboration with a friend, Geraldine Cummins' original compositions include only five complete books. The first, a novel, *The Land They Loved*, was written when she was twenty-eight; the second, also a novel, *The Fires of Beltane*, came out seventeen years later; she wrote her autobiography, *Unseen Adventures*, when she was sixty; her biography of her friend Edith Somerville followed a year later; finally a book of short stories presumably written before 1951, came out in 1959, entitled *Variety Show*.

The fact that she published so little original work, despite having cherished from her youth a wish to be an authoress, no doubt is largely to be explained by her concentration on her own psychic development after becoming acquainted with Hester Dowden, and on the practice of her automatism after she had taken up residence with Beatrice Gibbes.

Towards the end of 1951, a month before the latter died, she promised her that she would confine her energies to psychic work, but this alone does not explain why she published so little of her own original composition. The seventeen years' gap between the two novels suggests either a restriction in the flow of original ideas, an unwillingness on the part of publishers to produce her work, or a critical attitude on her own part towards her work which made her suppress most of it.

So were her creative faculties inhibited by her concentration on the psychic, or did she have the potential ability to become a skilful and successful writer of fiction?

A perusal of her two novels does show a certain development in skill. Both are on Irish themes; both are written from the point of view of a young country-bred Irishwoman; both are soaked in Irish styles of speech and Catholic Irish attitudes. The later novel shows a greater ability in handling the material than does the earlier. The first deals with a woman in her late twenties returning to her native village after many years in the United States where she worked as a cook. She has ideas about settling down as the wife of one of her two childhood sweethearts, both brothers - which, she does not know. But both are dead, one killed fighting for the British on the Western Front in the First World War, the other fighting the English in Dublin during the Easter Rising of 1916; before going to their respective dooms they had quarrelled bitterly over the different sides they had chosen to fight for. Their younger brother remains and wishes to marry her, but she rejects him for being too spiritless to stand up to his tyrannical father because he does not want to be disinherited from the family farm. She takes herself off to Dublin, finds a succession of jobs there, has various not very serious emotional adventures and in the end returns to her native area to find that the man she had rejected had now, after his father's death, become his own man at last and a vigorous asserter of the rights of the local people. Since he is a changed character she agrees to marry him; he is now more like his brothers had been. The plot is simple, the treatment episodic, the characters, in some cases, caricatures; it is not a very memorable book.

The second novel goes deeper and is rather more subtly written. The heroine, an attractive Irish girl, is wooed by a bucolic and unimaginative farmer, and everyone assumes they will make a match of it. But the girl prefers an aristocratic ne'er-do-well from the local big house and gives herself to him when he promises to marry her. Another woman detaches him from her so he deserts her and goes to the United States. Their child is born, and she then marries the farmer, but, like most Irish peasant marriages, it is one of convenience, not mutual love. She bears the latter a son, and the two boys eventually quarrel and one taunts the other with being a bastard. The book ends rather vaguely and inconclusively, with the older boy leaving home, going abroad and marrying a French girl; the heroine, now in her unattractive fifties, is left wondering about it all. There are sub-plots involving other characters,

THE NON-PSYCHIC WRITINGS

one an Irish fiddler and hedge-guru with a sister of appalling shrewishness who slits the throat of her brother's favourite tame crow out of jealousy for the affection he gives it. The whole is played out against the background of Irish Catholic sentiment and observance and the local priest, Father Flood, supplies a ground bass accompaniment of suitable religious comment.

I did not find either book made a compelling read, and kept remembering the Irish stories, set in a similar milieu, of Edith Somerville and Martin Ross. Geraldine did not have the quick sparkling wit of these two women writers. The texture of her writing is thicker; the characters do not stand out stereoscopically as those of Somerville and Ross; it is all suet and no soufflé. One cannot doubt that she knows well what she writes about; the settings and speech seem genuine. But there is no sparkle or scintillation. So it seems to me; to an Irish person it might appear otherwise.

The autobiography, while necessary reading for any later biographer, did not, I found, do much more than convey information for subsequent processing. It is a matter of bits and pieces that don't make much of a pattern. The same might be said for the biography of Edith Somerville, which has a high proportion of quotations. Gifford Lewis, in her recent biography of Somerville and Ross, speaks critically of it and compares it with the 'Myers' scripts. 'Despite her affection for Edith and her collection of excellent material, it is awkwardly written, with clumsy constructions and a tired use of words.' I do not feel able to disagree.

I found the short stories more interesting. There are a dozen in the published collection, presumably chosen out of many produced in magazines, or not offered for publication, before the promise which she made to Beatrice Gibbes to concentrate on her psychic work. Each story is woven round a central idea. In the first, *The Tinker's Bag*, an intrusive *deus ex machina* makes its appearance at the end to tie the threads together; two spinster sisters are saved from different unwelcome fates by an unexpected sweepstake prize of £10,000. Another story somewhat stretches one's credulity. An elderly woman, busy working herself to the bone in order to save money against her son's return from abroad, fails to recognise him when he comes back, far gone with tuberculosis, and drives him from her door to die in the fields and be buried as a stranger; meanwhile she goes on waiting. In a third, a Cork woman, an old harridan with a vituperative tongue, has a feckless son who gets involved in petty crime, is put into prison, and after his discharge goes to the United States to pursue a similar mode of existence. The old woman considered suicide, but gives that up at the last moment. Eventually she is taken to hear a gipsy fortune-teller, who says her son is abroad and has become some kind of general. A friend of the old woman writes to America to obtain confirmation and receives a reply which makes it plain that the man is the 'general' of a gang of hoodlums. The friend visits the mother and pretends to read the letter to her. The latter is now on her deathbed and is not told the whole truth - only that her son is some sort of governor-general. The woman dies happy at her son's achievement of greatness.

One feels that the promise extracted by Beatrice Gibbes from Geraldine was perhaps for the best when one compares the quality of the non-psychical material with the quality of much of the automatic writing. One cannot certainly surmise that if Geraldine had not developed and used her psychic abilities she would never have made a name for herself in literature. But it is significant that, on her own admission, she wrote with great difficulty. Eight hundred words for an article could take a whole day. Was this because her mind became so adapted to writing automatically that it had to be bludgeoned into writing originally? Possibly Beatrice Gibbes realised that something like this was so. It is also significant that Geraldine kept her promise even after Beatrice's death, when she might have felt herself in some measure released from it.

It is possible, and even probable, that Geraldine would never have become a novelist of distinction if she had never met Mrs Hester Dowden in Paris and been diverted into mediumship. What is certain is that as a medium she ranks with the most celebrated of them all, both in quality and quantity of output. As with John Wesley, the world was to be her parish, and it is arguable that she helped more people in distress through bereavement than she would have entertained as a writer of fiction. No doubt, in the final analysis, it is the people we benefit and not the plaudits we receive which reap the greater spiritual harvest.

BIBLIOGRAPHY
BOOKS BY GERALDINE CUMMINS

*   1912 Broken faith: a play, S. R. Day & G. D. Cummins
*   1917 Fox and Geese: a Comedy, S. R. Day & G. D. Cummins
    1919 The Land They Loved: a Novel
** 1928 The Scripts of Cleophas
    1932 The Road to Immortality
    1935 Beyond Human Personality
    1936 The Fires of Beltane: a Novel
** 1937 The Childhood of Jesus
** 1939 When Nero was Dictator: St Paul's last years
    1946 They Survive: Geraldine Cummins & E. B. Gibbes
    1948 Travellers in Eternity
** 1949 The Manhood of Jesus: the unrecorded years of Christ's life
** 1950 I appeal unto Caesar
*   1951 Unseen Adventures: an Autobiography
*   1952 Dr E. Oe. Somerville: a Biography
    1955 The Fate of Colonel Fawcett
    1956 Mind in Life and Death
    1957 Healing the Mind: Geraldine Cummins & R. Connell
*   1959 Variety Show: Short stories
    1965 Swan on a Black Sea
** Undated Paul in Athens
** Undated The Great Days of Ephesus

*   Geraldine Cummins' non-psychic productions.
** Books in the Cleophas Script sequence.

BIBLIOGRAPHY

BOOKS REFERRED TO IN THE TEXT

Voices from the Void: H. Travers-Smith (Hester Dowden)
1953 *The Imprisoned Splendour:* Raynor C. Johnson
1968 *The Founders of Psychical Research:* Alan Gauld
1977 *Missing Persons:* E. R. Dodds
1983 *A Hand in Dialogue:* C. E. J. Fryer
1989 *The Decisive Testimony:* Raynor C. Johnson

Paperbacks also available from White Crow Books

Elsa Barker—*Letters from a Living Dead Man*
ISBN 978-1-907355-83-7

Elsa Barker—*War Letters from the Living Dead Man*
ISBN 978-1-907355-85-1

Elsa Barker—*Last Letters from the Living Dead Man*
ISBN 978-1-907355-87-5

Richard Maurice Bucke—*Cosmic Consciousness*
ISBN 978-1-907355-10-3

Arthur Conan Doyle—*The Edge of the Unknown*
ISBN 978-1-907355-14-1

Arthur Conan Doyle—*The New Revelation*
ISBN 978-1-907355-12-7

Arthur Conan Doyle—*The Vital Message*
ISBN 978-1-907355-13-4

Arthur Conan Doyle with Simon Parke—*Conversations with Arthur Conan Doyle*
ISBN 978-1-907355-80-6

Meister Eckhart with Simon Parke—*Conversations with Meister Eckhart*
ISBN 978-1-907355-18-9

D. D. Home—*Incidents in my Life Part 1*
ISBN 978-1-907355-15-8

Mme. Dunglas Home; edited, with an Introduction, by Sir Arthur Conan Doyle—*D. D. Home: His Life and Mission*
ISBN 978-1-907355-16-5

Edward C. Randall—*Frontiers of the Afterlife*
ISBN 978-1-907355-30-1

Rebecca Ruter Springer—*Intra Muros: My Dream of Heaven*
ISBN 978-1-907355-11-0

Leo Tolstoy, edited by Simon Parke—*Forbidden Words*
ISBN 978-1-907355-00-4

Leo Tolstoy—*A Confession*
ISBN 978-1-907355-24-0

Leo Tolstoy—*The Gospel in Brief*
ISBN 978-1-907355-22-6

Leo Tolstoy—*The Kingdom of God is Within You*
ISBN 978-1-907355-27-1

Leo Tolstoy—*My Religion: What I Believe*
ISBN 978-1-907355-23-3

Leo Tolstoy—*On Life*
ISBN 978-1-907355-91-2

Leo Tolstoy—*Twenty-three Tales*
ISBN 978-1-907355-29-5

Leo Tolstoy—*What is Religion and other writings*
ISBN 978-1-907355-28-8

Leo Tolstoy—*Work While Ye Have the Light*
ISBN 978-1-907355-26-4

Leo Tolstoy—*The Death of Ivan Ilyich*
ISBN 978-1-907661-10-5

Leo Tolstoy—*Resurrection*
ISBN 978-1-907661-09-9

Leo Tolstoy with Simon Parke—*Conversations with Tolstoy*
ISBN 978-1-907355-25-7

Howard Williams with an Introduction by Leo Tolstoy—*The Ethics of Diet: An Anthology of Vegetarian Thought*
ISBN 978-1-907355-21-9

Vincent Van Gogh with Simon Parke—*Conversations with Van Gogh*
ISBN 978-1-907355-95-0

Wolfgang Amadeus Mozart with Simon Parke—*Conversations with Mozart*
ISBN 978-1-907661-38-9

Jesus of Nazareth with Simon Parke—*Conversations with Jesus of Nazareth*
ISBN 978-1-907661-41-9

Thomas à Kempis with Simon Parke—*The Imitation of Christ*
ISBN 978-1-907661-58-7

Julian of Norwich with Simon Parke—*Revelations of Divine Love*
ISBN 978-1-907661-88-4

Allan Kardec—*The Spirits Book*
ISBN 978-1-907355-98-1

Allan Kardec—*The Book on Mediums*
ISBN 978-1-907661-75-4

Emanuel Swedenborg—*Heaven and Hell*
ISBN 978-1-907661-55-6

P.D. Ouspensky—*Tertium Organum: The Third Canon of Thought*
ISBN 978-1-907661-47-1

Dwight Goddard—*A Buddhist Bible*
ISBN 978-1-907661-44-0

Michael Tymn—*The Afterlife Revealed*
ISBN 978-1-970661-90-7

Michael Tymn—*Transcending the Titanic: Beyond Death's Door*
ISBN 978-1-908733-02-3

Guy L. Playfair—*If This Be Magic*
ISBN 978-1-907661-84-6

Guy L. Playfair—*The Flying Cow*
ISBN 978-1-907661-94-5

Guy L. Playfair—*This House is Haunted*
ISBN 978-1-907661-78-5

Carl Wickland, M.D.—*Thirty Years Among the Dead*
ISBN 978-1-907661-72-3

John E. Mack—*Passport to the Cosmos*
ISBN 978-1-907661-81-5

Peter & Elizabeth Fenwick—*The Truth in the Light*
ISBN 978-1-908733-08-5

Erlendur Haraldsson—*Modern Miracles*
ISBN 978-1-908733-25-2

Erlendur Haraldsson—*At the Hour of Death*
ISBN 978-1-908733-27-6

Erlendur Haraldsson—*The Departed Among the Living*
ISBN 978-1-908733-29-0

Brian Inglis—*Science and Parascience*
ISBN 978-1-908733-18-4

Brian Inglis—*Natural and Supernatural: A History of the Paranormal*
ISBN 978-1-908733-20-7

Ernest Holmes—*The Science of Mind*
ISBN 978-1-908733-10-8

Victor Zammit—*Afterlife: A Lawyer Presents the Evidence.*
ISBN 978-1-908733-22-1

Casper S. Yost—*Patience Worth: A Psychic Mystery*
ISBN 978-1-908733-06-1

William Usborne Moore—*Glimpses of the Next State*
ISBN 978-1-907661-01-3

William Usborne Moore—*The Voices*
ISBN 978-1-908733-04-7

John W. White—*The Highest State of Consciousness*
ISBN 978-1-908733-31-3

Stafford Betty—*The Imprisoned Splendor*
ISBN 978-1-907661-98-3

Paul Pearsall, Ph.D. —*Super Joy*
ISBN 978-1-908733-16-0

All titles available as eBooks, and selected titles available in Hardback and Audiobook formats from www.whitecrowbooks.com